FOREVER DUSTY

A MUSICAL BY
Kirsten Holly Smith
& Jonathan Vankin

Forever Dusty (1st ed. - 08.07.15) - foreverdustyglm
Copyright © 2014 Kirsten Holly Smith and Jonathan Vankin

ALL RIGHTS RESERVED

Copyright Protection. This play (the "Play") is fully protected under the copyright laws of the United States of America and all countries with which the United States has reciprocal copyright relations, whether through bilateral or multilateral treaties or otherwise, and including, but not limited to, all countries covered by the Pan-American Copyright Convention, the Universal Copyright Convention, and the Berne Convention.

Reservation of Rights. All rights to this Play are strictly reserved, including, without limitation, professional and amateur stage performance rights; motion picture, recitation, lecturing, public reading, radio broadcasting, television, video, and sound recording rights; rights to all other forms of mechanical or electronic reproduction now known or yet to be invented, such as CD-ROM, CD-I, DVD, photocopying, and information storage and retrieval systems; and the rights of translation into non-English languages.

Performance Licensing and Royalty Payments. Amateur and stock performance rights to this Play are controlled exclusively by Playscripts, Inc. ("Playscripts"). No amateur or stock production groups or individuals may perform this Play without obtaining advance written permission from Playscripts. Required royalty fees for performing this Play are specified online at the Playscripts website (www.playscripts.com). Such royalty fees may be subject to change without notice. Although this book may have been obtained for a particular licensed performance, such performance rights, if any, are not transferable. Required royalties must be paid every time the Play is performed before any audience, whether or not it is presented for profit and whether or not admission is charged. All licensing requests and inquiries concerning amateur and stock performance rights should be addressed to Playscripts (see contact information on opposite page).

Inquiries concerning all other rights should be addressed to the author's agent: Susan R. Gurman, The Susan Gurman Agency, LLC, 865 West End Ave, New York, NY 10025 (phone: 212-749-4618; fax: 212-864-5055).

Restriction of Alterations. There shall be no deletions, alterations, or changes of any kind made to the Play, including the changing of character gender, the cutting of dialogue, the cutting of music, or the alteration of objectionable language, unless directly authorized by Playscripts. The title of the Play shall not be altered.

Author Credit. Any individual or group receiving permission to produce this Play is required to give credit to the author as the sole and exclusive author of the Play. This obligation applies to the title page of every program distributed in connection with performances of the Play, and in any instance that the title of the Play appears for purposes of advertising, publicizing, or otherwise exploiting the Play and/or a production thereof. The name of the author must appear on a separate line, in which no other name appears, immediately beneath the title and of a font size at least 50% as large as the largest letter used in the title of the Play. No person, firm, or entity may receive credit larger or more prominent than that accorded the author. The name of the author may not be abbreviated or otherwise altered from the form in which it appears in this Play.

Publisher Attribution. All programs, advertisements, and other printed material distributed or published in connection with the amateur or stock production of the Play shall include the following notice:

Produced by special arrangement with Playscripts, Inc.
(www.playscripts.com)

Prohibition of Unauthorized Copying. Any unauthorized copying of this book or excerpts from this book is strictly forbidden by law. Except as otherwise permitted by applicable law, no part of this book may be reproduced, stored in a retrieval system, or transmitted in any form, by any means now known or yet to be invented, including, without limitation, photocopying or scanning, without prior permission from Playscripts.

Statement of Non-affiliation. This Play may include references to brand names and trademarks owned by third parties, and may include references to public figures. Playscripts is not necessarily affiliated with these public figures, or with the owners of such trademarks and brand names. Such references are included solely for parody, political comment, or other permitted purposes.

Permissions for Sound Recordings and Musical Works. This Play may contain directions calling for the performance of a portion, or all, of a musical work *not included in the Play's score*, or performance of a sound recording of such a musical work. Playscripts has not obtained permissions to perform such works. The producer of this Play is advised to obtain such permissions, if required in the context of the production. The producer is directed to the websites of the U.S. Copyright Office (www.copyright.gov), ASCAP (www.ascap.com), BMI (www.bmi.com), and NMPA (www.nmpa.org) for further information on the need to obtain permissions, and on procedures for obtaining such permissions.

The Rules in Brief

1) Do NOT perform this Play without obtaining prior permission from Playscripts, and without paying the required royalty.
2) Do NOT photocopy, scan, or otherwise duplicate any part of this book.
3) Do NOT alter the text of the Play, change a character's gender, delete any dialogue, cut any music, or alter any objectionable language, unless explicitly authorized by Playscripts.
4) DO provide the required credit to the author(s) and the required attribution to Playscripts in all programs and promotional literature associated with any performance of this Play.

For more details on these and other rules, see the opposite page.

Copyright Basics

This Play is protected by United States and international copyright law. These laws ensure that authors are rewarded for creating new and vital dramatic work, and protect them against theft and abuse of their work.

A play is a piece of property, fully owned by the author, just like a house or car. You must obtain permission to use this property, and must pay a royalty fee for the privilege—whether or not you charge an admission fee. Playscripts collects these required payments on behalf of the author.

Anyone who violates an author's copyright is liable as a copyright infringer under United States and international law. Playscripts and the author are entitled to institute legal action for any such infringement, which can subject the infringer to actual damages, statutory damages, and attorneys' fees. A court may impose statutory damages of up to $150,000 for willful copyright infringements. U.S. copyright law also provides for possible criminal sanctions. Visit the website of the U.S. Copyright Office (www.copyright.gov) for more information.

THE BOTTOM LINE: If you break copyright law, you are robbing a playwright and opening yourself to expensive legal action. Follow the rules, and when in doubt, ask us.

Playscripts, Inc.
7 Penn Plaza, Suite 904
New York, NY 10001

toll-free phone: 1-866-NEW-PLAY
email: info@playscripts.com
website: www.playscripts.com

*To my family and friends.
Without your support, none of this would have been possible.*

-Kirsten Holly Smith

To my mom, Jean F. Vankin, who made everything possible.

-Jonathan Vankin

Cast of Characters

DUSTY SPRINGFIELD (aka MARY O'BRIEN), iconic 1960s British Pop star. English, though ethnically Irish. Age: 20s-30s.

JERRY WEXLER, veteran record producer, seen it all in the music industry. Age 51.

TOM SPRINGFIELD (aka DION O'BRIEN), Dusty's brother, older by four years. Excellent musician and songwriter.

BOB THACKERAY, English music journalist. 30s-40s.

BECKY BRIXTON, English television producer who becomes Dusty's manager. Approximately same age as Dusty.

CLAIRE BENNETT, African-American. Journalist. Late 20s through mid-30s; also depicted in her 50s.

MR. VANDER SANT, South African government official circa 1964. 40s or 50s.

RECORD EXECUTIVE, one of the most powerful men in the music business. 30s or 40s.

GINI, Dusty's drug and alcohol counselor and friend. 30s. New Age/former hippie.

SCHOOL GIRLS (2)

THE LANA SISTERS (2)

SOUL SINGER

STAGE MANAGER

SEXY WOMAN

DOCTOR

Production Notes

The story of *Forever Dusty* takes place over the course of Dusty Springfield's life, from her teen years in the 1950s until her passing at age 59. The major story elements occur in the 1960s and 1970s.

The action takes place in multiple settings. In the original Off-Broadway staging of *Forever Dusty*, scene changes were accomplished by use of projections.

The cast consisted of five actors, each playing multiple roles with the exception of Dusty, in the following configuration:

CAUCASIAN FEMALE 1: Dusty Springfield

CAUCASIAN FEMALE 2: Becky Brixton / Gini / School Girl 2 / Lana Sister / Sexy Woman

AFRICAN-AMERICAN FEMALE: Claire Bennett / Soul Singer / School Girl 1 / Lana Sister

CAUCASIAN MALE 1 (20s-30s): Tom Springfield / Record Executive

CAUCASIAN MALE 2 (40s-50s): Jerry Wexler / Bob Thackeray / South African Official / Stage Manager / Doctor

Acknowledgments

Forever Dusty received its world premiere Off-Broadway at New World Stages in a production directed by Randal Myler with the following cast and production staff:

DUSTY SPRINGFIELD . . . . Kirsten Holly Smith
CLAIRE. . . . . Christina Sajous
BOB / JERRY . . . . Benim Foster
TOM SPRINGFIELD . . . . Sean Patrick Hopkins
BECKY / GINI. . . . . Coleen Sexton
Understudies . . . . Ashley Betton, Jonathan C. Kaplan

Assistant Director . . . . Patrick Goss
Executive Producer / General Manager . . . Eva Price and
                                Maximum Entertainment
Producers . . . . Leslie Brockett, Jane Gullong,
                  Jorja Fox, Sandalphon Productions
Associate Producers . . . . Helga Olafsson and
                                 Lawrence D. Poster
Musical Direction /
    Arrangements . . . . Michael Thomas Murray
Choreography . . . . Jenny Lynn Spencer
Set Design. . . . . Wilson Chin
Costume Design . . . . Nancy Palmatier
Lighting and Projection Design . . . . Richard DiBella
Wig Design. . . . . Paul Huntley
Sound Design. . . . . Matt Kraus
Stage Manager. . . . . Kris Valentine
Company Manager . . . . Holly Sutton
Fight Director. . . . . Adam Kenneth Moss
Wardrobe Supervisor . . . . Jeannie Williams

All production groups performing this play are required to include the following credits on the title page of every program:

Forever Dusty
Book by Kirsten Holly Smith & Jonathan Vankin
Premiered at New World Stages in a production directed by Randal Myler
Produced by Leslie Brocket, Jane Gullong, Jorja Fox, Sandalphon Productions
Associate Producers Helga Olafsson and Lawrence D. Poster

Song Credits

"Wishin' and Hopin'" (Burt Bacharach / Hal David)

"Seven Little Girls Sitting In the Back Seat" (Bill Hilliard / Lee Pockriss)

"Island of Dreams" (Tom Springfield)

"Tell Him" (Bert Berns)

"I Only Want to Be With You" (Michael Edwin Hawker / Ivor Raymonde)

"The Look of Love" (Burt Bacharch / Hal David)

"Just a Little Lovin'" (Barry Mann / Cynthia Weil)

"People Get Ready" (Curtis Mayfield)

"Willie and Laura Mae Jones" (Tony Joe White)

"Love Power" (Teddy Vann)

"I Close My Eyes and Count to Ten" (Clive Westlake)

"Son of a Preacher Man" (John Hurley / Ronnie Wilkins)

"Little by Little" (Buddy Kaye / Bea Verdi)

"Crumbs Off the Table" (Ronald Dunbar / Edith Wayne / Sherrie Payne)

"I Just Don't Know What to Do With Myself" (Burt Bacharach / Hal David)

"What Have I Done To Deserve This" (Ailee Willis / Neil Tennant / Christopher Lowe)

"Brand New Me" (Thom Bell / Jerry Butler / Kenny Gamble)

"Quiet Please, There's a Lady On Stage" (Peter Allen / Carole Bayer Sager)

"I Found My Way" (Gil Slavin / Mike Soles)

"Don't Forget About Me" (Gerry Goffin / Carole King)

FOREVER DUSTY

book by Kirsten Holly Smith & Jonathan Vankin
music and lyrics by Various Composers

ACT I

Scene 1

(Memphis, 1968. Recording studio. Lights up on DUSTY SPRINGFIELD, *behind a microphone.*

She's classic 1960s Dusty, blond, sexy with her trademark heavy eye-liner and oversize false eyelashes, a self-aware pastiche of the big-screen glamour queens she worshipped as a teenager: Catherine Deneuve, Kim Novak, Monica Vitti.

Dusty is not a teenager anymore. She's a star, struggling not to fade.

JERRY WEXLER, *grizzled music biz veteran, sits at the studio control desk. Large glasses and a newsboy cap. This is the man who invented the phrase "rhythm and blues." Nothing that happens in a recording studio fazes him. But he's never worked with* DUSTY SPRINGFIELD. *Until now.*

They've been in this studio far longer than either wanted or planned.)

SONG: SON OF A PREACHER MAN

DUSTY.
BILLY RAY WAS A PREACHER'S SON
AND WHEN HIS DADDY WOULD VISIT HE'D COME ALONG
WHEN THEY GATHERED ROUND AND STARTED FLOCKIN'
THAT'S WHEN BILLY WOULD—

JERRY. Hold it! Dusty, stop.

DUSTY. Oh dear. What have I done now?

JERRY. Screwed up the words. Again.

DUSTY. Did I? Really?

JERRY. Yeah, it's "talkin'." "Gathered 'round and started talkin'." Not "flockin'."

DUSTY. Are you quite sure?

JERRY. "Flockin'" doesn't even make sense.

DUSTY. I'm terribly sorry. I usually write the words on my hands and wrists so when I'm performing I can—

(She throws up a few of her signature, sweeping hand gestures.)

—see them.

JERRY. Okay! *Dusty in Memphis.* "Son of a Preacher Man." Take twenty-six.

SONG: SON OF A PREACHER MAN

DUSTY. Has it really been that many?

(Music stops!)

JERRY. *Dusty in Memphis.* "Son of a Preacher Man." Take twenty-seven.

SONG: SON OF A PREACHER MAN

DUSTY.
BILLY RAY WAS A PREACHER'S SON
AND WHEN HIS DADDY WOULD VISIT—

Excuse me? Jerry? It's so cold in here. *Brrr!* Like London in winter. I'm afraid it's muffing up my vocals.

JERRY. It's not your vocals I'm worried about.

DUSTY. What's that?

JERRY. Don't worry, hang on a second. I'll take care of it.

(JERRY sits down, lights a cigarette. Waits a moment.)

JERRY. Okay, I turned up the thermostat. Is that better?

DUSTY. I think so. Thanks so much.

JERRY. *Dusty in Memphis.* "Son of a Preacher Man." Take twenty-eight.

SONG: SON OF A PREACHER MAN

DUSTY.
BILLY RAY WAS A PREACHER'S SON
AND WHEN HIS DADDY WOULD VISIT HE'D COME ALONG
WHEN THEY GATHERED—

Jerry, the tempo's too fast! What is this? The bloody Grand Prix? *(To band:)* You're not getting it!

JERRY. Dusty, these cats are the Memphis Cats. The Memphis Sound is their sound. They invented it.

DUSTY. And I'm just a middle-class white girl from England.

JERRY. Well…

DUSTY. It's fine, Jerry. No, you can say it. It's true. These blokes have played for Aretha, Isaac, Otis. Now they're reduced to playing for —who's that girl who thinks she can sing our music? Oh, yes. Dusty Springfield!

JERRY. Dusty! Pull it together, Honey. Trust us. Just—sing.

DUSTY. Jerry, I can't. I want to, more than anything. But I can't sing the way you want me to.

JERRY. All right, everyone. Call it a night. We'll get back at this later.

DUSTY. No, no, Jerry. I'm sorry. I'll get it! I think I'm getting it now. Please don't leave. Jerry, please?

> *(But* JERRY *is gone.* THE MEMPHIS CATS *drop their instruments, exhausted, disgusted and done for the night. Dawn breaks.* DUSTY *hails a taxi.)*

DUSTY. Peabody Hotel. Please. If you would be so kind. Your name is Samuel, is it? My name is—Mary.

Scene 2

> *(Gray post-war England. St. Ann's School for Girls. Schoolyard at recess, presided over by stern nuns.*
> DUSTY *is now* MARY. *She slips on thick, black horn-rimmed glasses.)*

NUN. *(Voiceover:)* Mary Isobel Catherine Bernadette O'Brien!

MARY. Coming, Sister!

> *(A sharp recess whistle!*
> MARY *rushes into line. She stands at attention with other girls. She sneaks a peek at the backside of the girl next to her.)*

GIRL 1. What you lookin' at, O'Brien?

> *(Another whistle. The girls relax.)*

GIRL 2. She ain't even got a voice, does she?

MARY. No, I do.

GIRL 1. I heard a scandalous rumor that she sings.

MARY. Occasionally. In the bath.

GIRL 2. Let's hear it, then. Sing for us.

MARY. I'll be in trouble with the sisters if I do.

GIRL 2. You'll be in trouble with us if you don't.

(GIRL 1 *moves closer, flirty.*)

GIRL 1. We'd love it if you would.

SONG: WISHIN' AND HOPIN'

(*As the song opens,* MARY *is painfully shy, barely singing at all. As the number continues,* MARY *comes to life and wins the girls over completely.*)

MARY.
WISHIN' AND HOPIN'
AND THINKIN' AND PRAYIN'
PLANNIN' AND DREAMIN'
EACH NIGHT OF HIS CHARMS,
THAT WON'T GET YOU INTO HIS ARMS.

SO IF YOU'RE LOOKING TO FIND LOVE YOU CAN SHARE.
ALL YOU GOTTA DO IS HOLD HIM AND KISS HIM
AND LOVE HIM AND SHOW HIM THAT YOU CARE.

SHOW HIM THAT YOU CARE JUST FOR HIM,
DO THE THINGS HE LIKES TO DO,
WEAR YOUR HAIR JUST FOR HIM,
CAUSE YOU WON'T GET HIM
THINKIN' AND A PRAYIN',
WISHIN' AND A HOPIN'.

MARY & GIRLS.
CAUSE WISHIN' AND HOPIN'
AND THINKIN' AND PRAYIN',
PLANNIN' AND DREAMIN'
HIS KISSES WILL START,

MARY.	**GIRLS.**
THAT WON'T GET YOU INTO HIS HEART.	AH-OOH
SO IF YOU'RE THINKING OF HOW GREAT TRUE LOVE IS. ALL YOU GOTTA DO IS	AH AH AH

MARY & GIRLS.
HOLD HIM AND KISS HIM
AND SQUEEZE HIM, AND LOVE HIM, YEAH
JUST DO IT AND AFTER YOU DO,
YOU WILL BE HIS.

MARY.   **GIRLS.**

YOU GOTTA SHOW HIM THAT YOU CARE	DOO DOO DO DOO DOO
JUST FOR HIM	DOO DOO DO DOO DOO
AND DO THE THINGS HE LIKES TO DO	DOO DOO DO DOO DOO
	DOO DOO DO DOO DOO
WEAR YOUR HAIR	DOO DOO DO DOO DOO
JUST FOR HIM	DOO DOO DO DOO DOO
CAUSE YOU WON'T GET HIM THINKIN' AND A PRAYIN' WISHING' AND A HOPIN'	

MARY & GIRLS.
    'CAUSE WISHIN' AND HOPIN'
    AND THINKIN' AND PRAYIN'
    PLANNIN' AND DREAMIN'
    HIS KISSES WILL START,

MARY.   **GIRLS.**

THAT WON'T GET YOU INTO HIS HEART.	AH-OOH
SO IF YOU'RE THINKING OF HOW GREAT TRUE LOVE IS.	AH
	AH AH
ALL YOU GOTTA DO IS	

MARY & GIRLS.
    HOLD HIM AND KISS HIM
    AND SQUEEZE HIM, AND LOVE HIM, YEAH
    JUST DO IT AND AFTER YOU DO,
    YOU WILL BE HIS

    (The other GIRLS *exit.)*

Scene 3

(O'Brien family home. A modest, middle class place. Mary's brother DION *enters, with guitar. Slightly annoyed, he tries to tune and play.)*

MARY.
    WISHIN' AND HOPIN'
    THINKIN' AND PRAYIN'
    PLANNIN' AND DREAMIN'

DION. Mary, would you mind?

MARY. Oh, Dion. I didn't notice you there.

DION. I can't imagine why not.

MARY. Dad's scheduled a lesson with me later. I needed to practice.

DION. Practice for your practice?

MARY. It's Dad.

DION. Yes, well, I know what that's like. In any case, I've got a melody that's just popped into my head, so if I could have quiet for a few moments...

> (MARY *waits, fidgety, as* DION *plays his tune. She can barely contain herself. The tune is a rudimentary version of "Island of Dreams.")*

DION.
HIGH IN THE SKY IS THE BIRD ON THE WING
PLEASE TAKE ME WITH—

(Thinks:)

PLEASE *CARRY* ME—

MARY. I'll sing it with you!

DION. I haven't finished it yet, Mary.

> *(The voices of Dusty's father, O.B., and mother, KAY, are heard from off stage.)*

O.B. *(Offstage:)* You're off to France again? You don't even speak bloody French!

KAY. *(Offstage:)* Maybe this time I'll learn.

> *(Door slams.*
>
> DION *places a comforting, big-brotherly arm around his sister.)*

MARY. It's my fault. I upset Dad yesterday.

DION. Mary, they don't need a reason to argue.

MARY. I don't know how I'd survive without you, Dion.

DION. *(Teasing:)* You wouldn't, of course.

> *(They share a smile.* DION *hands a newspaper to* MARY.*)*

DION. Look, this may brighten your spirits.

MARY. "Girl group seeks backup singer. The Lana Sisters." Dion, do you think I'm ready?

DION. Not with these.

(DION *takes* MARY's *glasses off of her face. She squints, nearly blind.*)

DION. Now you're ready.

(MARY *hesitates.*)

DION. Go on, now. When they hear your voice, well—just go!

Scene 4

(*Audition room. A basement somewhere.* DION *watches, silent but proud.*)

AUDITIONER. *(Voiceover:)* Next!

(MARY *steps forward carefully.*)

Name!

MARY. O'Brien. Mary O'Brien.

AUDITIONER. *(Voiceover:)* Louder!

MARY. Mary O'Brien. Hello.

SONG: WISHIN' AND HOPIN'

MARY.
YOU GOTTA SHOW HIM THAT YOU CARE JUST FOR HIM
AND DO THE THINGS HE LIKES TO DO
WEAR YOUR HAIR JUST FOR HIM

'CAUSE YOU WON'T GET HIM
THINKIN' AND A PRAYIN'

AUDITIONER. *(Voiceover, cuts her off:)* Thank you!

(*A lengthy, nerve-wracking pause.*)

Well, when can you start?

Scene 5

(*Music hall at an English holiday resort camp. The late 1950s.*)

AUDITIONER. *(Voiceover:)* Ladies and gentlemen, good evening and welcome to Butlin's Holiday Camp on the lovely seashore in Blackpool! For your entertainment this evening, Butlin's proudly presents Britain's new girl group sensation—The Lana Sisters!

(MARY *and the other two "sisters" enter.*)

SONG: SEVEN LITTLE GIRLS SITTING IN THE BACK SEAT

ALL GIRLS.
ALL TOGETHER NOW, 1.2.3.
KEEP YOUR MIND ON YOUR DRIVING, KEEP YOUR HANDS ON THE WHEEL
KEEP YOUR SNOOPY EYES ON THE ROAD AHEAD
WE'RE HAVIN' FUN, SITTIN' IN THE BACK SEAT
KISSIN' AND A HUGGIN' WITH FRED
DEE DOOD DEE DOOM DOOM
DEE DOOD-DEE DOOM DOOM
DEE DOOD-DEE DOOM DOOM DOO

(DION *enters.*)

DION. *(Enthusiastically:)* Bravo! Encore!

MARY. Dion! What are you doing here?

DION. I came to see my sister—the pop star.

MARY. Oh, please.

DION. But there's one thing. Why don't you call me Tom from now on?

MARY. Well, all right. Tom.

(*Awkward silence.*)

Why am I calling you Tom?

(DION *is now referenced as* "TOM.")

TOM. Because I'm starting my own group!

MARY. Your own group? That's fantastic, Dion. Tom.

TOM. I'll write the songs. But I need a lead singer. A stage presence. I know how you can sing and, well, look at you!

(MARY *looks toward her "sisters."*)

MARY. We have songs on the charts. A tour.

TOM. They're not really your sisters, you know. But I am your brother.

MARY. I'd love to join your group! What are you—what are *we* calling ourselves?

TOM. Remember how we used to look at the maps of America? In Dad's atlas?

MARY. Yes?

TOM. And we'd pick out these loads of American towns all with the same name?

MARY. Yes, I suppose.

TOM. We're calling ourselves "The Springfields!" It just sounds so *American,* you know. I'm Tom. And you…?

MARY. Remember how I used to play football with the boys?

TOM. Yes?

MARY. And these boys used to knock me on my arse, time after time?

TOM. Yes, I suppose. *(Gets it:)* Oh! They called you—

MARY. Dusty!

>   *(With that,* MARY *is now* "DUSTY.")

DUSTY & TOM. Dusty Springfield!

Scene 6

>   *(A TV Studio.* STAGE MANAGER *enters. Hands* TOM *his guitar.)*

STAGE MANAGER. Remember, big smiles, kids. Our sponsor, Mother's Pride Bread, is in the audience tonight. Big smiles! Big! And you're on in five, four—

>   *(*STAGE MANAGER *counts down with hand signals.)*

SONG: ISLAND OF DREAMS

DUSTY & TOM.
>   I WANDER THE STREETS AND THE GAY CROWDED PLACES
>   TRYING TO FORGET YOU BUT SOMEHOW IT SEEMS
>   MY THOUGHTS EVER STRAY TO OUR LAST SWEET EMBRACES
>   OVER THE SEA ON THE ISLAND OF DREAMS

DUSTY.
>   HIGH IN THE SKY IS THE BIRD ON THE WING
>   PLEASE CARRY ME WITH YOU

DUSTY & TOM.
>   FAR FAR AWAY FROM THE MAD RUSHING CROWD
>   PLEASE CARRY ME WITH YOU
>
>   AGAIN I WOULD WANDER WHERE MEMORIES ENFOLD ME
>   THERE ON THE BEAUTIFUL ISLAND OF DREAMS

FAR FAR AWAY ON THE
ISLAND OF DREAMS

Scene 7

(New York, 1963. DUSTY enters Colony Records store. TOM is with her, but off on his own with his own agenda.)

DUSTY. "Far, far away, on my island of dreams…"

(Her thoughts are broken by the raucous opening bars of…)

SONG: TELL HIM

(The sound stops her. She's never been so excited!)

DUSTY. Excuse me, Sir? Sorry. It's my very first time in America. We're here on tour with our group. The Springfields?

(Nothing coming back.)

Yes, well. Anyway. What *is* this record you're playing?

(Female R&B SINGER enters.)

DUSTY. "Tell Him." The Exciters!

SINGER.
I KNOW SOMETHING ABOUT LOVE
YOU'VE GOTTA WANT IT BAD
IF THAT GUY'S GOT INTO YOUR BLOOD
GO OUT AND GET HIM

SINGER.	**BACKUP.**
	DOOT DOO DOO,
IF YOU WANT HIM TO BE	DOOT DOO DOO
	DOOT DOO DOO
THE VERY THOUGHT OF YOU	DOOT DOO DOO
	DOOT DOO DOO
MAKES YOU WANT TO BREATHE	DOOT DOO DOO
	DOOT DOO DOO
HERE'S THE THING TO DO	DOOT DOO DOO

SINGER & BACKUP.
TELL HIM THAT YOU'RE NEVER GONNA LEAVE HIM
TELL HIM THAT YOU'RE ALWAYS GONNA LOVE HIM
TELL HIM, TELL HIM, TELL HIM
TELL HIM RIGHT NOW

DUSTY. Oh, Tom! Doesn't it leave you breathless?

(TOM's *not a fan.*)

DUSTY. The attack on it! We don't have anything like this in England!

> (*Overwhelmed with the magnitude of her discovery, from this moment* DUSTY's *life has changed.* DUSTY *moves to the music. As the song continues, she loosens up and moves less like a Lana Sister and more like a soul singer.*)

SINGER.
> I KNOW SOMETHING ABOUT LOVE
> YOU GOTTA SHOW IT AND
> MAKE HIM SEE THE MOON UP ABOVE
> GO OUT AND GET HIM
> IF YOU WANT HIM TO
> MAKE YOUR HEART SING OUT
> IF YOU WANT HIM TO
> ONLY THINK OF YOU

SINGER & BACKUP.
> TELL HIM THAT YOU'RE NEVER GONNA LEAVE HIM
> TELL HIM THAT YOU'RE ALWAYS GONNA LOVE HIM
> TELL HIM, TELL HIM, TELL HIM
> TELL HIM RIGHT NOW

> (TOM *checks his watch, forces a smile.*)

DUSTY. The least you can do is act like you enjoy it.

TOM. I'm sorry. Not my scene, I'm afraid.

SINGER.
> I KNOW SOMETHING ABOUT LOVE
> YOU GOTTA TAKE HIS HAND
> SHOW HIM WHAT THE WORLD IS MADE OF
> ONE KISS WILL PROVE IT

DUSTY.
> IF YOU WANT HIM TO BE
> ALWAYS BY YOUR SIDE
> TAKE HIS HAND TONIGHT
> SWALLOW YOUR FOOLISH PRIDE

DUSTY / SINGER / BACKUP.
> TELL HIM THAT YOU'RE NEVER GONNA LEAVE HIM
> TELL HIM THAT YOU'RE ALWAYS GONNA LOVE HIM
> TELL HIM, TELL HIM, TELL HIM
> TELL HIM RIGHT NOW

> (*Tune continues, underscore.*)

TOM. Look, I've nothing against this R&B music. But this is not The Springfields' sound.

DUSTY. But Tom, I think this is my sound!

TOM. Your sound? If you haven't noticed, the people singing this music that you love so much, well—

(*Music suddenly stops.*)

—they're black.

(TOM *looks around, mortified that someone heard that.*)

DUSTY. I've had an offer. *Ready Steady Go!* It's a program on telly.

TOM. I know what it is. You mean you're booking our television appearances now?

DUSTY. No.

TOM. Good. That's my job, you know.

DUSTY. It's not The Springfields that received the offer, Tom. It's me.

TOM. What? Solo? That's not possible. Without you, The Springfields are finished. We have songs on the charts. A tour!

DUSTY. I'm sorry, Tom.

TOM. It's not your decision.

DUSTY. But it is.

TOM. If you end the group, we're finished.

DUSTY. I know.

TOM. (*More sad than angry:*) I don't mean the group. I mean you and me. Dion and Mary. You shan't hear from me again.

DUSTY. I love this music, Dion.

(TOM/DION *gives her one last look. He turns and walks out of her life.* DUSTY *stands alone—with her future.*)

Scene 8

(*A cramped London TV studio, the home of* Ready Steady Go!

BECKY BRIXTON *enters, urgent.*)

BECKY. Dusty! Where the hell is she?

STAGE MANAGER. (*Offstage:*) Ninety seconds to air. Miss Brixton, you're the producer. You've got to get her out there.

BECKY. Yes, yes! *(To herself:)* I've got to bloody find her first. Dusty!

    (DUSTY enters.)

DUSTY. Coming! Coming! Sorry! Sorry!

BECKY. Dusty, you're not dressed yet.

DUSTY. I can't do this, Becky. I can't do this alone.

BECKY. You'd better. Or London will be looking at three minutes of dead air. *Ready Steady Go!* is live!

DUSTY. An encouraging word might not kill you.

STAGE MANAGER. *(Voiceover:)* One minute to air!

BECKY. We have clocks in here, thank you!

DUSTY. What if my wig falls off?

BECKY. Hair pins.

DUSTY. My throat! What if my voice completely goes?

BECKY. Sucrets.

DUSTY. Or my stockings run?

BECKY. Seamless micro-mesh. Guaranteed run-proof.

DUSTY. My God! I forgot to feed the cat!

    (She begins heaving, about to lose her lunch. She finds a wastepaper bin.)

DUSTY. I really thought I could do this alone. But I can't! I just can't. I—I...

STAGE MANAGER. *(Offstage:)* Thirty seconds to air!

    (DUSTY's about to lose it right into the trash bin! But BECKY yanks it away.)

BECKY. You're not getting out of this that easily.

    (DUSTY turns green.)

BECKY. You're on!

    (BECKY exits. DUSTY is alone, looking in the mirror.)

DUSTY. The bigger the hair, the blacker the eyes, the more I can hide.

    (Music starts, underscore.)

ANNOUNCER. *(Voiceover:)* All right, boys and girls, the weekend starts here on *Ready Steady Go!* Here she is, in her solo telly debut— Dusty Springfield!

(DUSTY rushes to the stage.)

SONG: I ONLY WANT TO BE WITH YOU

(The moment the music starts, it's as if DUSTY *were born under spotlights.)*

DUSTY.	BACKUP.
I DON'T KNOW WHAT IT IS	AH
THAT MAKES ME LOVE YOU SO.	LOVE YOU SO
I ONLY KNOW I NEVER WANT	AH
TO LET YOU GO,	LET YOU GO
'CAUSE YOU STARTED SOMETHING,	AH, AH
OH, CAN'T YOU SEE	AH, AH
THAT EVER SINCE WE MET	AH
YOU HAD A HOLD ON ME?	AH
IT HAPPENS TO BE TRUE	
I ONLY WANT TO	ONLY WANT TO
BE WITH YOU.	BE WITH YOU
IT DOESN'T MATTER WHERE	AH
YOU GO OR WHAT YOU DO,	WHAT YOU DO
I WANT TO SPEND EACH MOMENT	AH
OF THE DAY WITH YOU.	DAY WITH YOU
OH, LOOK WHAT HAS HAPPENED	AH, AH
WITH JUST ONE KISS.	AH, AH
I NEVER KNEW THAT I COULD	AH
BE IN LOVE LIKE THIS.	AH
IT'S CRAZY BUT IT'S TRUE,	
I ONLY WANT TO	ONLY WANT TO
BE WITH YOU.	BE WITH YOU
YOU STOPPED AND SMILED AT ME,	
ASKED IF I CARE TO DANCE.	
I FELL INTO YOUR OPEN ARMS	
AND I DIDN'T STAND A CHANCE!	
NOW, LISTEN HONEY,	
I JUST WANT TO BE	AH
BESIDE YOU EVERYWHERE	EVERYWHERE
AS LONG AS WE'RE TOGETHER,	AH
HONEY, I DON'T CARE.	I DON'T CARE
'CAUSE YOU STARTED SOMETHING,	AH, AH
OH, CAN'T YOU SEE	AH, AH
THAT EVER SINCE WE MET	AH
YOU HAD A HOLD ON ME?	AH
NO MATTER WHAT YOU DO,	

I ONLY WANT TO BE WITH YOU.	ONLY WANT TO BE WITH YOU
WHOA OH OOH OH OH YOU STOPPED AND SMILED AT ME, ASKED IF I CARE TO DANCE. I FELL INTO YOUR OPEN ARMS AND I DIDN'T STAND A CHANCE!	
	I DIDN'T STAND A CHANCE!

NOW HEAR ME TELL YA,
I JUST WANT TO BE
BESIDE YOU EVERYWHERE
AS LONG AS WE'RE TOGETHER,
    HONEY, I DON'T CARE.
'CAUSE YOU STARTED SOMETHING,
    OH, CAN'T YOU SEE
THAT EVER SINCE WE MET
YOU HAD A HOLD ON ME?
I ONLY WANT TO BE WITH YOU.
	
	AH
	EVERYWHERE
	AH
	I DON'T CARE
	AH, AH
	AH, AH
	AH
	AH

I SAID NO MATTER,
NO MATTER WHAT YOU DO

DUSTY & BACKUP.
I ONLY WANT TO BE WITH
I ONLY WANT TO BE WITH
I ONLY WANT TO BE WITH YOU!

(*As the music plays off,* DUSTY *basks for a moment in her triumph. She exits.*)

Scene 9

(*London's Rainbow Theatre, teeming with kids.* BECKY *enters.* BOB THACKERAY *trails behind her, observing.*)

BECKY. You there! Get off your arse and reset those lights! Dusty's on next!

THACKERAY. Congratulations, Brixton. The first Motown revue in the UK and it's a smashing success.

BECKY. What are you getting at, Thackeray?

THACKERAY. Well, if you don't mind my saying, you seem a little tense.

BECKY. This show was all Dusty's idea really. You'd be tense too if you were answering to her.

    (DUSTY *enters, relaxed, happy.*)

BECKY. *(All smiles.)* Dusty! I'd like to introduce—

THACKERAY. Bob Thackeray, Miss Springfield. *Daily Mail.*

DUSTY. I know your writing well, Mr. Thackeray. I'm so pleased you're here tonight.

THACKERAY. Yes, well, I was wondering—you're both hosting and lending your name to this revue, at which all of the performers are American and colored. Are you concerned how the British public might respond?

    (DUSTY *approaches* BOB *as if she's got a secret for him.*)

DUSTY. Here's my answer. *(He leans in.)* Stuff the British public!

    (BOB *gets a chuckle out of that. He puts pen to notepad.*)

DUSTY. Oh, don't write that down.

THACKERAY. Any pop star willing to tell the British public to stuff it deserves not to be quoted.

DUSTY. Bob, these musicians are my friends—my *idols.* Let's just— enjoy their performances.

THACKERAY. Fair enough.

    (THACKERAY *exits, thoroughly amused by this character.* CLAIRE BENNETT *enters, head down, scribbling her notepad.*)

    (CLAIRE *is African-American, approximately Dusty's age, strikingly beautiful, businesslike.*)

    (DUSTY *walks toward* BECKY—*and crashes into* CLAIRE!)

DUSTY. Oh! Excuse me.

CLAIRE. Excuse you!

DUSTY. I'm sorry. Journalists are seated—

    (*She's struck by* CLAIRE's *beauty.*)

DUSTY. —in the fourth row.

CLAIRE. You don't look like no press agent, Sugar.

BECKY. Look here, Miss.

CLAIRE. I'm with *Down Beat.* *(To* DUSTY:*)* Heard of it?

    (DUSTY *waves* BECKY *off.* BECKY *exits.*)

DUSTY. I have. And why is an American jazz magazine sending a reporter to write about Motown acts in England?

CLAIRE. It isn't.

DUSTY. Oh, really? Then may I ask, why are you here?

CLAIRE. You may.

(A silence. CLAIRE enjoys this.)

CLAIRE. I dig your outfit.

DUSTY. Thank you.

CLAIRE. Little old to be dressing like one of those teenage mod girls, aren't you?

DUSTY. Old? No, you see, *they* are dressing like *me*. Silly. I know. Your answer to my question. Why are you here?

CLAIRE. Same as you. To hear this Motown sound for myself.

DUSTY. But these songs are all over the charts in America.

CLAIRE. But I don't live in America. I'm living in Copenhagen right now. Stockholm before that. And a little in Paris and Nice.

DUSTY. You must have quite a story behind your travels.

CLAIRE. Back in the States, no one cares about jazz. All the best players go to Europe. So I moved to Europe.

DUSTY. I would give anything to live in America.

CLAIRE. Haven't you seen what's going on in Mississippi? Alabama? Doesn't that make the news here?

DUSTY. Yes, of course. I don't pay much attention to newspapers.

CLAIRE. America don't want people like me.

DUSTY. You haven't told me your name.

(Music begins. Underscore.)

DUSTY. I'm sorry, it seems to be my time to sing.

CLAIRE. In *this* show?

DUSTY. Yes. It appears so.

SONG: THE LOOK OF LOVE

DUSTY. You'll stay to hear me?

CLAIRE. I've got a deadline. So…

DUSTY. I'd love it if you would.

CLAIRE. Claire. My name's Claire.

DUSTY. Claire.

> *(DUSTY rushes to the "stage.")*

ANNOUNCER. *(Offstage:)* And now, ladies and gentlemen, your hostess—Dusty Springfield!

> *(CLAIRE is impressed. Stunned. She can't stop watching DUSTY.)*

DUSTY.
> THE LOOK OF LOVE
> IS IN YOUR EYES,
> THE LOOK YOUR HEART
> CAN'T DISGUISE.
>
> THE LOOK OF LOVE
> IS SAYING SO MUCH MORE
> THAN JUST WORDS COULD EVER SAY.
> AND WHAT MY HEART HAS HEARD,
> WELL, IT TAKES MY BREATH AWAY.
>
> I CAN HARDLY WAIT TO HOLD YOU,
> FEEL MY ARMS AROUND YOU.
> HOW LONG I HAVE WAITED—
> WAITED JUST TO LOVE YOU
> NOW THAT I HAVE FOUND YOU.

CLAIRE.
> YOU'VE GOT THE LOOK OF LOVE
> IT'S ON YOUR FACE
> A LOOK THAT TIME
> CAN'T ERASE.
>
> BE MINE TONIGHT
> LET THIS BE JUST THE START OF
> SO MANY NIGHTS LIKE THIS.
> LET'S TAKE A LOVER'S VOW
> AND THEN SEAL IT WITH A KISS

DUSTY & CLAIRE.
> I CAN HARDLY WAIT TO HOLD YOU,
> FEEL MY ARMS AROUND YOU.
> HOW LONG I HAVE WAITED—
> WAITED JUST TO LOVE YOU
> NOW THAT I HAVE FOUND YOU
> DON'T EVER GO.
> DON'T EVER GO.
> I LOVE YOU SO.

(DUSTY and CLAIRE exit, hand in hand.)

Scene 10

(A few days later. Dusty's flat. A swanky, swinging London pad. CLAIRE, in a robe, types madly on a manual Smith-Corona. DUSTY, also in a robe, enters.)

(Music underscore throughout.)
SONG: JUST A LITTLE LOVIN'

CLAIRE. Just got one last deadline.

DUSTY. Work, work, work. I work all the time. Not you too.

CLAIRE. Not all the time. Obviously.

DUSTY. JUST A LITTLE LOVIN'

CLAIRE. Dusty…

DUSTY.
EARLY IN THE MORNIN'
BEATS A CUP OF COFFEE
FOR STARTIN' OUT THE DAY

CLAIRE.
JUST A LITTLE LOVIN'
WHEN THE WORLD IS YAWNIN'
MAKES YOU WAKE UP FEELIN' GOOD THINGS
ARE COMING YOUR WAY

DUSTY & CLAIRE.
THIS OLD WORLD
IT WOULDN'T BE HALF AS BAD
IT WOULDN'T BE HALF AS SAD
IF EACH AND EVERYBODY IN IT HAD

DUSTY. I didn't know I owned a typewriter.

CLAIRE. This girl's mine. I had her shipped the other day.

DUSTY. Oh. Then—you'll be staying a while?

(They hug.)

Darling, that makes me so—happy!

CLAIRE. Dusty, you sure this is cool? The newspapers? The gossip?

DUSTY. Oh, please. The newspapers have me sleeping with Burt Bacharach. That's *this* week. Last week they had me turning down McCartney, but jumping into bed with Jagger.

CLAIRE. Oh God.

DUSTY. Oh God. *(Beat.)* Love, there's something I must tell you.

CLAIRE. You can tell me anything, Baby.

DUSTY. In a few days from now, I'm leaving.

CLAIRE. Wait—what?

DUSTY. On a tour, Darling. That's all! Just a couple of weeks. An international tour.

CLAIRE. I'll come with you. I travel for work all the time. *(Reads DUSTY's reaction.)* Oh. I dig.

DUSTY. No, it isn't *that*. It's not that at all. I swear. I'm only looking out for you, Claire. You must know, I can't bear to be apart from you even for—

CLAIRE. Shhh. A few days from now ain't now.

DUSTY & CLAIRE.
THIS OLD WORLD
IT WOULDN'T BE HALF AS BAD
IT WOULDN'T BE HALF AS SAD
IF EACH AND EVERYBODY IN IT HAD

DUSTY.
JUST A LITTLE LOVIN'
EARLY IN THE MORNIN'

CLAIRE.
JUST A LITTLE LOVIN'
WHEN THE WORLD IS YAWNIN'

DUSTY & CLAIRE.
JUST A LITTLE LOVIN'
EARLY IN THE MORNIN'
JUST A LITTLE BIT OF LOVIN'

Scene 11

(Dusty's flat. Evening. BECKY is there. DUSTY is poised to sign a contract.)

CLAIRE. When you said "international" you didn't say you were going to *South Africa*.

BECKY. Dusty, please, sign the bloody contract.

(DUSTY *moves pen toward paper.* CLAIRE *shoves her hand in the way.*)

CLAIRE. You don't know what you're up against, Girl.

BECKY. She has everything sorted!

DUSTY. Becky! Claire, I have everything sorted.

BECKY. Dusty. May I speak with you a moment? Privately.

DUSTY. Whatever you need to say to me, Becky, you can say to Claire as well.

BECKY. Fine. You've trusted me for almost two years. Have you been disappointed yet?

DUSTY. Of course not.

BECKY. Six hit singles? A Top 10 LP? *New Musical Express* female performer of the year?

DUSTY. Becky, where is this leading?

CLAIRE. It's okay, Dusty. She's right. Why should you listen to me?

DUSTY. Never say that, Claire.

CLAIRE. Just ask yourself something. Why do you want to perform in that country?

DUSTY. I just want everyone who digs my music to be able to come and hear me sing it.

CLAIRE. But not everyone *can* come hear you sing it. Unless by "everyone," you mean "everyone white."

DUSTY. That's unfair. I will never perform to a segregated audience.

BECKY. It's right here, in black and white.

CLAIRE. Why are you being so naive?

BECKY. My God. She is many things. But naive? I think not.

DUSTY. God damn it, Becky! Claire, I won't sing for a segregated audience. It's my promise to you.

(DUSTY *signs the paperwork.*)

CLAIRE. Dusty, it's apartheid.

Scene 12

(South Africa. DUSTY on stage.)

DUSTY. Hello, Cape Town! It's such a delight to be here tonight and to see so many beautiful faces, together as one.

SONG: PEOPLE GET READY / WILLIE AND LAURA MAE JONES

DUSTY. I hope these songs will inspire you, all of you, to dream about true community and friendship that sees no color.

>PEOPLE GET READY, THERE'S A TRAIN A COMIN'
>YOU DON'T NEED NO BAGGAGE, YOU JUST GET ON BOARD
>ALL YOU NEED IS FAITH TO HEAR THE DIESELS HUMMIN'
>DON'T NEED NO TICKET, YOU JUST THANK THE LORD

>WILLIE AND LAURA MAE JONES
>WERE OUR NEIGHBORS A LONG TIME BACK
>THEY LIVED RIGHT DOWN THE ROAD FROM US
>IN A SHACK JUST LIKE OUR SHACK.

>THE PEOPLE WORKED THE LAND TOGETHER
>AND WE LEARNED TO COUNT ON EACH OTHER.
>WHEN YOU LIVE OFF THE LAND YOU DON'T HAVE THE
>   TIME TO
>THINK ABOUT ANOTHER MAN'S COLOR.

DUSTY & BACKUP.
>THE COTTON WAS HIGH AND
>THE CORN WAS GROWIN' FINE,

DUSTY.	**BACKUP.**
BUT THAT WAS ANOTHER PLACE	OOH
AND ANOTHER TIME.	OOH OOH
SIT OUT ON THE FRONT PORCH	
IN THE EVENING WHEN	
THE SUN WENT DOWN.	YEAH
WILLIE WOULD PLAY AND	
THE KIDS WOULD SING	
AND EVERYBODY WOULD MESS AROUND.	
DADDY'D BRING OUT HIS GUITAR	
AND PLAY ON THROUGH	
THE NIGHT.	YEAH
EVERY NOW AND THEN	
OLD WILLIE WOULD GRIN	
AND SAY, "HEY, YOU PLAY ALRIGHT."	

>*(Spoken:)* Made me feel so good!

I REMEMBER THE BEST TIMES OF ALL
WHEN SATURDAY CAME AROUND,　　OOH OOH
WE ALL WOULD STOP BY　　　　　　OOH OOH
    WILLIE'S HOUSE
AND SAY, "DO YA'LL NEED　　　　　OOH OOH
    ANYTHING FROM TOWN?"

HE'D SAY, "NO, BUT WHY DON'T　　OOH OOH
YA'LL STOP ON THE WAY　　　　　　OOH OOH
    BACK THROUGH?
AND I'LL GET LAURA MAE, YEAH,
TO COOK UP SOME BARBECUE.

(Spoken:) And you know that's good!

DUSTY & BACKUP.
THE COTTON WAS HIGH AND
THE CORN WAS GROWIN' FINE,

DUSTY.　　　　　　　　　　　　　**BACKUP.**
YES IT WAS
BUT THAT WAS ANOTHER PLACE　　OOH

AND ANOTHER TIME.　　　　　　　OOH OOH

THE YEARS ROLLED PAST THE LAND
AND TOOK BACK WHAT
    THEY'VE GIVEN.　　　　　　　YEAH
WE ALL KNEW WE HAD TO MOVE
IF WE WERE GONNA MAKE A LIVIN'
SO WE ALL MOVED OFF
AND WENT ABOUT OUR
    SEPARATE WAYS　　　　　　　YEAH
IT SURE WAS HARD TO SAY GOOD-BYE
TO WILLIE AND LAURA MAE　　　　JONES!
OH, YEAH...

DUSTY & BACKUP.
THE COTTON WAS HIGH AND
THE CORN WAS GROWIN' FINE,

DUSTY.
YES IT WAS

DUSTY & BACKUP.
BUT THAT WAS ANOTHER PLACE AND ANOTHER TIME

DUSTY.　　　　　　　　　**BACKUP.**
I REMEMBER THE WAY　　　COTTON WAS HIGH AND
YEAH, OH　　　　　　　　　THE CORN WAS GROWIN' FINE

DUSTY.	BACKUP.
OH COTTON LOOKED SO FINE	
BUT THAT WAS ANOTHER PLACE	OOH
AND ANOTHER TIME	OOH OOH

DUSTY & BACKUP.
PEOPLE GET READY, THERE'S A TRAIN A COMIN'
YOU DON'T NEED NO BAGGAGE, YOU JUST GET ON BOARD
ALL YOU NEED IS FAITH TO HEAR THE DIESELS HUMMIN'
DON'T NEED NO TICKET

DUSTY.
YOU JUST THANK, OH YOU JUST THANK THE L—

POLICE OFFICER. *(Offstage:)* Stop! By order of the Cape Town City Police, this performance has been declared a threat to public safety!

(DUSTY *stands speechless, stunned.*)

Scene 13

(DUSTY's *hotel room. She argues with a South African official,* MR. VANDER SANT.
She eats a damp sandwich off a paper plate.)

DUSTY. Mr. Vander Sant! We've been confined to this hotel room for three days. Can I at least get a decent meal? A plate of bangers, even. If I look at one more bloody tomato sandwich, I'll vomit!

VANDER SANT. Please sign this document, Miss Springfield. Then we will be able to let you leave.

DUSTY. If I put my signature on that document, I lose whatever rights I have under my contract.

VANDER SANT. The contract is not valid.

DUSTY. My contract, Mr. Vander Sant, quite clearly states that we were to perform in cinemas because racially mixed audiences are not yet banned there. We held up our end of the bargain.

VANDER SANT. Mixed-race audiences violate South African law.

DUSTY. To hell with your laws! If I'm in violation of your law, deport me!

VANDER SANT. *(After a beat:)* If you are deported, the government is obligated to purchase your airline fare. And that's—expensive.

DUSTY. Expensive? Dear God, you're both evil and cheap!

VANDER SANT. All we ask is respect for tradition when you are in our country.

DUSTY. Respect?

VANDER SANT. Yes.

DUSTY. Tradition?

VANDER SANT. Yes.

DUSTY. Mr. Vander Sant, neither I nor anyone in my group is signing any piece of paper you place in front of us. Unless it's a receipt for a ticket out of this bloody backwards country. So unless you're looking to get your scrawny arse kicked by a former field hockey player, I suggest you arrange our travel and get the fuck out of my hotel room this instant!

Scene 14

(Heathrow airport. A pack of reporters. DUSTY *enters in coat and dark glasses.)*

GROUP OF REPORTERS. *(Voiceover, ad lib:)* Miss Springfield! Dusty! Over here! Just one question!

REPORTER ONE. *(Voiceover:)* Dusty, was your stance against the South African government just a stunt to get your name in the papers?

DUSTY. Look, if you believe this was a publicity stunt, you're out of your mind. I need this kind of publicity like a hole in the head. In fact, I may sue the South African government. If they want to sling mud around, they've picked the wrong person. I have a far more deadly aim.

*(*DUSTY *exits.)*

Scene 15

(Dusty's flat. CLAIRE *talks on the phone. A TV is on in the background.)*

CLAIRE. I'm saying Coltrane's made another leap forward, like he did with "Giant Steps."

FEMALE TV PRESENTER. *(Voiceover:)* Pop star Dusty Springfield arrived at Heathrow this morning, direct from Cape Town, where her actions have caused a row between Britain and the government of South Africa.

CLAIRE. I'll call you back.

FEMALE TV PRESENTER. *(Voiceover:)* Actor Derek Nimmo, in particular has strong views on the Springfield situation.

(CLAIRE hangs up, troubled by what she hears on TV.)

DEREK NIMMO. *(TV Voiceover:)* There's no question that her actions were foolish and irresponsible.

(DUSTY enters, exhausted.)

DEREK NIMMO. *(TV Voiceover:)* Miss Springfield has certainly achieved an enormous step backward as far as the cause of racial equality—

(CLAIRE switches off the TV. DUSTY stands speechless. Mortified.)

CLAIRE. I'm really sorry, Dust.

DUSTY. *(Bravely:)* Never mind. It's only Nimmo. What a prat! *(Pours vodka.)* I was trying to bring people together. They're portraying me like some kind of villain.

(DUSTY washes down a pill. CLAIRE takes the drink from DUSTY, sets it down.)

CLAIRE. Come on, Dusty. It's not even noon.

DUSTY. Oh, please. I flew for more than 12 hours through the night and— *(Off CLAIRE's look:)* You're right. As always, Darling. You're right.

(Doorbell rings.)

DUSTY. They've come for me in my own home! Give me back that vodka!

(CLAIRE warily answers the door. Standing there—BOB THACKERAY.)

CLAIRE. May I help you?

THACKERAY. Oh. I am at the right flat, aren't I?

DUSTY. Is that Bob Thackeray?

(She collects herself, dries her eyes.)

DUSTY. Come in, Bob. Of course. Won't you sit down?

THACKERAY. No need, Dusty. Thank you. Didn't want to bother you at Heathrow. Just a couple of questions, then I'll be on my way.

DUSTY. This is my—dear friend. Claire.

THACKERAY. Pleasure.

(He extends his hand. CLAIRE shakes it, skeptical.)

DUSTY. How may I help you, Bob?

THACKERAY. Just wondering. All the money you earned from this tour—

DUSTY. —is going to charity. I don't want one penny.

THACKERAY. So, the South African government claims that you were warned not to perform in front of integrated crowds, but you deliberately chose to defy their orders.

DUSTY. You make it sound so dramatic.

THACKERAY. Did you think anything good could come out of this?

CLAIRE. She stood up to oppression.

DUSTY. Yes, there was one good thing. As I was boarding the plane home, a small group of airport porters, all black men, removed their berets in salute forming a solemn guard of honor.

CLAIRE. In their country, that's the highest display of respect.

DUSTY. Bob, honestly, it was the most sincere form of respect that I've ever known.

THACKERAY. Brilliant.

DUSTY. Be kind to me, will you, Bob?

THACKERAY. Always, Miss Springfield.

(He exits.)

CLAIRE. I don't get it, Baby. They kill you in the press, so you let them into our house?

DUSTY. I should have listened to you, Claire. I truly believed I was doing the right thing.

CLAIRE. You listened to your heart. I'm proud of you. *(Beat.)* Sometimes I wish I'd stood up for myself, instead of running away to Europe.

DUSTY. You didn't run away. You came to me. I would never have had the strength to do what I did without you.

CLAIRE. Promise me we'll go there soon, together, to America.

DUSTY. But, I thought you said America didn't want you?

CLAIRE. That's why I have to go.

(A pregnant beat.)

DUSTY. We'll go wherever you like!

SONG: LOVE POWER

DUSTY.
> WHEN WE WALK
> DOWN THE STREET
> WE DON'T CARE WHO WE SEE
> OR WHO WE MEET

CLAIRE.
> DON'T HAVE TO RUN
> DON'T HAVE TO HIDE
> 'CAUSE WE GOT SOMETHING
> BURNING INSIDE

DUSTY & CLAIRE.
> WE GOT LOVE POWER
> IT'S THE GREATEST POWER OF THEM ALL
> WE GOT LOVE POWER
> AND TOGETHER WE CAN'T FALL

CLAIRE.	**BACKUP.**
SOMETIMES WE'RE UP	AH AH
DUSTY.	
SOMETIMES WE'RE DOWN	AH AH
DUSTY & CLAIRE.	
BUT OUR FEET ARE ALWAYS	AH AH
ON THE GROUND	AH AH
DUSTY.	
WE ALWAYS LAUGH	AH AH
CLAIRE.	
DON'T HAVE TO CRY	AH AH
DUSTY & CLAIRE.	**BACKUP.**
AND THIS IS THE	AND THIS IS THE
REASON WHY	REASON WHY
WE GOT LOVE	LOVE
POWER	POWER
IT'S THE GREATEST POWER	HEY
OF THEM ALL	HEY,
HEY, HEY, HEY	HEY HEY HEY
WE GOT LOVE	LOVE
POWER	POWER
AND TOGETHER WE CAN'T FALL	

DUSTY / CLAIRE / BACKUP.
　　WE GOT LOVE, HEY, LOVE POWER
　　IT'S THE GREATEST FEELING OF THEM ALL
　　HEY, HEY, HEY
　　WE GOT LOVE, OH, POWER
　　AND TOGETHER WE CAN'T FALL

Scene 16

(London recording studio. DUSTY *listens through a bulky headset.* BECKY *stands by, impatiently.)*

DUSTY. No, no, no, Becky, it's still wrong.

BECKY. Dusty, I'll get Johnny. You really should speak to him about this.

DUSTY. Stuff Johnny. Stuff all English recording producers. They've been doing things the right and proper way for 30 years. You know they're not going to listen to some bee-hived bird.

BECKY. Trouble at home? You know, with *her.*

DUSTY. Are you referring to Claire?

BECKY. What is the trouble, then?

DUSTY. Him. The bass player.

BECKY. The bass player.

DUSTY. He's striking the strings with a plectrum.

BECKY. The right and proper way.

DUSTY. In America they play with their fingers. That is the sound I want.

BECKY. You! Drop that plectrum.

DUSTY. Becky, I can always count on you for the delicate touch.

BECKY. At your service, as always.

DUSTY. Once more. *(Listens:)* Bloody hell, Becky! The sound is so muddy, I've heard cleaner sound rumbling up a creaky lift! I need echo in the vocal. *(Sighs, disgusted:)* I'll be in the loo. And I don't care how many dirty looks I get. I need to feel like I'm living in the sound.

　　(DUSTY *sits, as if on the toilet.)*

DUSTY. Living in the—sound. MMM-mmm-mmm. MMM-MMM-MMMM! Oh my God, it's perfect sound in the bloomin' loo! Get in there, boys! Grab that other mic and swing it over the stall. Becky, if

I get a hit single out of this, who cares if I recorded it in the ladies' toilet?

SONG: I CLOSE MY EYES AND COUNT TO TEN

Scene 17

(TV Studio. DUSTY sings "live.")

ANNOUNCER. *(Voiceover:)* From the BBC TV Theatre in Shepherd's Bush, London, it's—*The Dusty Springfield Show!*

DUSTY.
>IT ISN'T THE WAY THAT YOU LOOK
>AND IT ISN'T THE WAY THAT YOU TALK
>IT ISN'T THE THINGS THAT YOU SAY OR DO
>MAKE ME WANT YOU SO

DUSTY & BACKUP.
>IT HAS NOTHING TO DO WITH THE WINE
>OR THE MUSIC THAT'S FLOODING MY MIND

DUSTY.
>BUT NEVER BEFORE HAVE I BEEN SO SURE
>YOU'RE THE SOMEONE I DREAMED I WOULD FIND
>
>IT'S THE WAY YOU MAKE ME FEEL
>THE MOMENT I AM CLOSE TO YOU
>IT'S A FEELING SO UNREAL
>SOMEHOW I CAN'T BELIEVE IT'S TRUE

DUSTY & BACKUP.
>THE POUNDING I FEEL IN MY HEART
>THE HOPING THAT WE'LL NEVER PART

DUSTY.
>I CAN'T BELIEVE THIS IS REALLY HAPPENING TO ME
>
>I CLOSE MY EYES AND COUNT TO TEN

DUSTY.	**BACKUP.**
AND WHEN I OPEN THEM	
YOU'RE STILL HERE	AH
I CLOSE MY EYES AND	AH
COUNT AGAIN	

DUSTY & BACKUP.
>I CAN'T BELIEVE IT BUT YOU'RE STILL HERE

DUSTY.
WE WERE

DUSTY & BACKUP.
    STRANGERS A MOMENT AGO
    WITH A FEW DREAMS BUT NOTHING TO SHOW

DUSTY.
    THE WORLD WAS A PLACE
    WITH A FROWN ON ITS FACE
    AND TOMORROW WAS JUST, I DON'T KNOW

    BUT THE WAY YOU MAKE ME FEEL
    THE MOMENT I AM CLOSE TO YOU
    MAKES TODAY SEEM SO UNREAL
    SOMEHOW I CAN'T BELIEVE IT'S TRUE

DUSTY & BACKUP
    TOMORROW WILL YOU STILL BE HERE?
    TOMORROW WILL COME, BUT I FEAR

DUSTY.
    THAT WHAT IS HAPPENING TO ME
    IS ONLY A DREAM

    I CLOSE MY EYES AND COUNT TO TEN

DUSTY.	**BACKUP.**
AND WHEN I OPEN THEM	
YOU'RE STILL HERE	AH
I CLOSE MY EYES AND	AH
COUNT AGAIN	

DUSTY & BACKUP.
    I CAN'T BELIEVE IT BUT YOU'RE STILL

DUSTY.	**BACKUP.**
HERE	AH
I CLOSE MY EYES AND	AH
COUNT AGAIN	

DUSTY & BACKUP.
    I CAN'T BELIEVE IT BUT YOU'RE STILL

DUSTY.	**BACKUP.**
HERE	AH

    (DUSTY *takes a bow and exits.*)

Scene 18

(Dusty and Claire's flat. CLAIRE *is mesmerized by images on TV. The U.S. Civil rights struggle.* CLAIRE *crouches on one knee, scribbling intently in a reporter's notebook.*
Dr. Martin Luther King speaks on TV.
CLAIRE *pockets down her notes and stands, in awe, deeply moved.)*

DR. KING. *(Voiceover:)* We've got to find a method that will disrupt our cities if necessary, create the crisis that will force the nation to look at the situation, dramatize it, and yet at the same time not destroy life or property. You know what I see that as? I see that as massive civil disobedience.

*(*DUSTY *enters and pours a drink.)*

DUSTY. My favorite color. Vodka.

CLAIRE. Dusty, have you thought—I don't know—that it's time for a change?

DUSTY. That's exactly what I've been telling you, Darling. When I hear the *new* music, *Rubber Soul,* Bob Dylan—my God, "You Don't Have to Say You Love Me" sounds like the theme from *Ben Hur.*

CLAIRE. Things are changing back home. I'm changing too.

DUSTY. Oh, Claire. I don't want you to change. You look great.

CLAIRE. You're not listening.

DUSTY. Yes, I am, Claire. Of course I am.

(Awkward silence.)

DUSTY. What is it?

CLAIRE. America, Dusty. Have you given it any thought?

DUSTY. I've thought about it. It's about time I give those blokes at Phillips Records a right talking to. Their promotional efforts over there have been shameful.

CLAIRE. Are you doing this on purpose?

DUSTY. What's that, Love?

CLAIRE. Bringing everything back to yourself, when I'm talking about something—bigger?

DUSTY. I hate it when we argue, Darling!

CLAIRE. Dusty, I've spent too long running away. I'm going home. To America.

DUSTY. Are you saying—you're leaving?

CLAIRE. No. I mean, yes. But I want you with me. I need to—I don't know—write about it. Or just be there. When I had the chance—I just ran. No more.

DUSTY. Well—I know something about that.

CLAIRE. Dusty, I can't let what's happening there happen without me. I have to go home.

DUSTY. Then I swear to you. I will get us there.

Scene 19

(The office of a big-time American RECORD EXECUTIVE. *He's a powerful man and he knows it.* DUSTY *strides in, confident as she can pretend to be.)*

DUSTY. Good afternoon. I'm Dusty Springfield. I'll say it right out. I would be honored to sign with your label.

EXECUTIVE. Slow down, Honey. Welcome to the Big Apple.

DUSTY. I have—

EXECUTIVE. How was your flight?

DUSTY. I have—

EXECUTIVE. You want a drink?

DUSTY. I have only one condition.

EXECUTIVE. Guess I'm drinking alone. *(Pouring drink:)* It's good to relax before talking business. That's my belief. Get to know each other.

DUSTY. Jerry Wexler.

EXECUTIVE. Okay, you win. *(Takes a sip.)* What about him?

DUSTY. He has recorded all of the great soul artists. I will record with him as my producer and no one else.

EXECUTIVE. I think we can market you that way. A crossover thing. Blacks and whites buying the same album.

DUSTY. Exactly!

EXECUTIVE. Sounds good to me.

DUSTY. I'm delighted you agree.

EXECUTIVE. Sure. But one thing. If I let you have Jerry, what do you have for me?

DUSTY. I'm sorry?

EXECUTIVE. I've followed your career for several years now. I always thought you were a very attractive girl.

DUSTY. Right. If you want to cash in on my unique crossover appeal, as you say, let's make this deal. If not, I'm fully prepared to walk straight out that door and find another American label.

EXECUTIVE. Can't blame a man for trying.

>   (*He signs a piece of paper and hands it to* DUSTY, *who grabs it.*)

Scene 20

>   (*A room in the Plaza Hotel, New York.* CLAIRE *writes on a note pad.* DUSTY *enters with the contract.*)

DUSTY. Claire, you would have been so proud of me! I just held my ground with the most powerful man in the recording business.

CLAIRE. Yeah?

DUSTY. Shy Mary O'Brien could never have done that. She would have been flat on her back with her knickers around her ankles.

CLAIRE. What?

DUSTY. But not Dusty Springfield. She stood strong and proud—on her own two feet!

CLAIRE. Whoa, back it up. Rewind it, Dusty. What the hell happened?

DUSTY. I signed my first American recording contract.

>   (CLAIRE *reaches for the document.*)

DUSTY. You don't want to read this boring thing. We should throw a party!

CLAIRE. Come on, let me see. This is a big deal.

>   (DUSTY *reluctantly hands it over. She pours a drink.*)

CLAIRE. Dusty this is incredible. "To be produced by *Jerry Wexler*... American Sound Studios... (*Beat.*) "Memphis...?"

DUSTY. (*Puts on her best happy face:*) Here's to *Dusty in Memphis*.

CLAIRE. Baby. Anywhere but Memphis.

DUSTY. I brought us to America, as I promised.

CLAIRE. After what they did to Dr. King, I won't set foot in that town.

DUSTY. It wasn't my choice, Claire. Jerry says we must record in the same studio as Aretha, Otis and, well, all of the original musicians. Frankly, I'm terrified. *(More booze.)* You're scared, too. I understand.

CLAIRE. Do you? Really?

DUSTY. No, I suppose I don't. Still, I'm asking you, Claire, please come with me. I can't do this alone.

CLAIRE. It's just for a few weeks. You won't be alone.

DUSTY. No? I am quite alone, wouldn't you say? Does every journalist ask you if you're bent? Must you pretend to be forever on the hunt for a husband? No one cares who you sleep with. No one cares who you love.

CLAIRE. *(Fighting tears:)* Go to Memphis, Dusty. You'll be fine. *(Grabs a sweater, heads out.)* When you get back, we'll see if this still works.

DUSTY. That hurts.

CLAIRE. You're hurting yourself. But you do that, don't you?

DUSTY. Where are you going?

CLAIRE. For a walk through the park. Alone.

>   (DUSTY, *alone, stares at the empty space where* CLAIRE *used to be.)*

Scene 21

>   *(1968. Memphis recording studio.* DUSTY *is at the mic.* JERRY *is at the controls in the booth.)*

JERRY. *Dusty in Memphis.* "Son of a Preacher Man." Take forty-seven!

SONG: SON OF A PREACHER MAN

(The musicians don't get far.)

DUSTY. Stop, God Damn it! Jerry, The sound's not right. The beat is sloppy, my voice is weak. And this song. She wants to make love with a preacher's son? Does that sound like anything I've ever experienced?

JERRY. Enough of this shit!

DUSTY. Oh, God. Who nicked my pills? Right, then. I'd like a drink. These things tend to sound better when you're pissed. A God damned Grand Marnier would suit me right now.

JERRY. Do what I tell you and finish this track!

DUSTY. Bollocks, Jerry!

JERRY. Listen Sweetie, I've done this a few times before, you know. *(To the band:)* We never got this crap from Aretha. Did we, boys? Now she was a real professional.

DUSTY. Is that it, then? All this is because I have a producer who's a prima donna?

JERRY. There's only one prima donna in this studio.

(DUSTY *hurls an ashtray at him. A stunned silence follows.*)

DUSTY. I'm sorry. Jerry, I'm terribly embarrassed.

JERRY. Okay. It's all right. Wow. We're going to make a hell of a record here. All you gotta do is sing.

DUSTY. Not here. I'm sorry, Jerry. Not in Memphis. I need to go back to New York.

JERRY. Let me understand what you're saying. You want to record this album, *Dusty in Memphis*, in New York City?

Scene 22

(New York. A few weeks later. Recording studio.)

JERRY. *Dusty in Memphis.* "Son of a Preacher Man." New York City. Take—one!

SONG: SON OF A PREACHER MAN

(CLAIRE *enters, joining* JERRY *in the booth.* DUSTY *launches into the song. This time, she sounds amazing.*)

DUSTY.
BILLY RAY WAS A PREACHER'S SON
AND WHEN HIS DADDY WOULD VISIT HE'D COME ALONG.
WHEN THEY GATHERED ROUND AND STARTED TALKIN'
THAT'S WHEN BILLY WOULD TAKE ME WALKIN'
ALL THROUGH THE BACK YARD WE'D GO WALKIN'
THEN HE'D LOOK INTO MY EYES,
LORD KNOWS TO MY SURPRISE!

THE ONLY ONE WHO COULD EVER REACH ME

DUSTY & BACKUP.
WAS THE SON OF A PREACHER MAN.

DUSTY.
THE ONLY BOY WHO COULD EVER TEACH ME

DUSTY & BACKUP.
WAS THE SON OF A PREACHER MAN.

DUSTY. **BACKUP.**
YES, HE WAS, HE WAS, MM, YES HE WAS...

BEIN' GOOD ISN'T ALWAYS EASY,
NO MATTER HOW HARD I TRY. OOH OOH
WHEN HE STARTED SWEET TALKIN' TO ME
HE'D COME AND TELL ME
EVERYTHING IS ALRIGHT. OOH OOH
HE'D KISS AND TELL ME
EVERYTHING IS ALRIGHT. OOH OOH
CAN I GET AWAY AGAIN TONIGHT?

THE ONLY ONE WHO COULD EVER REACH ME

DUSTY & BACKUP.
WAS THE SON OF A PREACHER MAN.

DUSTY.
THE ONLY BOY WHO COULD EVER TEACH ME

DUSTY & BACKUP.
WAS THE SON OF A PREACHER MAN.

DUSTY. **BACKUP.**
YES, HE WAS, WAS
HE WAS, WAS
LORD KNOWS HE WAS...

HOW WELL I REMEMBER,
THE LOOK THAT WAS IN HIS EYES,
STEALIN' KISSES FROM ME ON THE SLY,

DUSTY & BACKUP.
TAKIN' TIME TO MAKE TIME,
TELLIN' ME HE WAS ALL MINE,
LEARNING' FROM EACH OTHER'S KNOWIN'
LOOKING TO SEE HOW MUCH WE'VE GROWN.

DUSTY.
AND THE ONLY ONE WHO COULD EVER REACH ME

DUSTY & BACKUP.
WAS THE SON OF A PREACHER MAN.

DUSTY.
THE ONLY BOY WHO COULD EVER TEACH ME

DUSTY & BACKUP.
WAS THE SON OF A PREACHER MAN.

DUSTY.
    YES, HE WAS,
    HE WAS,

BACKUP.
    WAS
    WAS
    OH YES HE WAS

    HOW WELL I REMEMBER,   HOW WELL I REMEMBER

DUSTY.
    THE LOOK THAT WAS IN HIS EYES,
    STEALIN' KISSES FROM ME ON THE SLY,

DUSTY & BACKUP.
    TAKIN' TIME TO MAKE TIME,
    TELLIN' ME HE WAS ALL MINE,
    LEARNING' FROM EACH OTHER'S KNOWIN'
    LOOKING TO SEE HOW MUCH WE'VE GROWN.

DUSTY.
    THE ONLY ONE WHO COULD EVER REACH ME

DUSTY & BACKUP.
    WAS THE SON OF A PREACHER MAN.

DUSTY.
    THE ONLY BOY WHO COULD EVER TEACH ME

DUSTY & BACKUP.
    WAS THE SON OF A PREACHER MAN.

DUSTY.
    YES, HE WAS,
    HE WAS,
    OH YES HE WAS

BACKUP.
    WAS
    WAS
    OOH

    THE ONLY ONE WHO
    COULD EVER REACH ME

DUSTY.
    HE WAS THE SWEET-
        TALKIN'
    SON OF A PREACHER MAN

BACKUP.
    WAS THE
    SON OF A PREACHER MAN

    THE ONLY BOY WHO
    COULD EVER TEACH ME

    AH, KISS ME   WAS THE
    SON OF A PREACHER MAN   SON OF A PREACHER MAN

    WAS   WAS
    WAS   WAS
    OH LORD,   OOH
    YES HE WAS   WAS

(Triumph! CLAIRE *looks on with the old pride that she always felt.* DUSTY *looks to* JERRY, *eager for his approval.)*

JERRY. *(With a shrug:)* That'll work.

Scene 23

(The Record Exec's office. 1970. The EXECUTIVE *is in the middle of lunch.)*

DUSTY. "Not available in the current catalog?"

EXECUTIVE. There's no question. *Dusty in Memphis* is a great album. Destined to be a classic. I couldn't be more proud.

DUSTY. And...?

EXECUTIVE. There was one small problem. No one bought it.

DUSTY. *Rolling Stone* wrote a rave review. People loved *Dusty in Memphis.*

EXECUTIVE. Not people. *(Beat.)* Critics.

DUSTY. My music brings people together.

EXECUTIVE. Things changed. White audiences hear the black sound and all they hear is, "Kill the honky." Black audiences see a white face and they see—well, you know what they see.

DUSTY. But that's not who I am.

SONG: LITTLE BY LITTLE

EXECUTIVE. This is the 70s now, Kid. Be someone new.

*(*DUSTY *sings to the* EXECUTIVE.*)*

DUSTY.
LITTLE BY LITTLE BY LITTLE BY LITTLE BY LITTLE
LITTLE BY LITTLE BY LITTLE BY LITTLE BY LITTLE.
YOU'RE MESSIN' UP MY LIFE
TEARING ME APART,
BREAKING UP MY WORLD
BY GIVING UP MY HEART
OOOOH LITTLE BY LITTLE BY LITTLE BY LITTLE.

*(*DUSTY *exits.)*

Scene 24

(Song continues. Scene shifts from New York to Los Angeles. Dusty's Laurel Canyon villa. A lesbian party. CLAIRE enters — followed by a SEXY WOMAN who gulps a cocktail.)

CLAIRE.
I'M LOSING ALL MY PRIDE.
IT'S REALLY GETTIN' BAD.
HURTING DEEP INSIDE —
IT'S MAKING ME GO MAD
OOOOH LITTLE BY LITTLE BY LITTLE BY LITTLE.
LITTLE BY LITTLE,
BIT BY BIT,
I'M GOING CRAZY AND YOU'RE CAUSING IT.
LITTLE BY LITTLE,
BIT BY BIT,
I SHOULD STOP CARING BUT MY LOVE WON'T QUIT.

I DON'T KNOW WHERE TO TURN.
I DON'T KNOW WHAT TO DO.
WALKING ON THIN ICE
IT SEEMS LIKE I'M FALLING THROUGH.
OOOOH LITTLE BY LITTLE
LITTLE BY LITTLE

(DUSTY re-enters. With CLAIRE watching, she flirts with the SEXY WOMAN.)

DUSTY.
I'M THE QUEEN OF FOOLS,
YOU KNOW THE DECK IS STACKED.
I'M ON A LOSING STREAK
BUT I'M GONNA GET YOU BACK
OOOOH LITTLE BY LITTLE BY LITTLE BY LITTLE
LITTLE BY LITTLE, LITTLE BY LITTLE

DUSTY / CLAIRE / SEXY WOMAN.
LITTLE BY LITTLE BY LITTLE BY LITTLE BY LITTLE
OOOOH LITTLE BY LITTLE BY LITTLE BY LITTLE
LITTLE BY LITTLE BY LITTLE BY LITTLE BY LITTLE!

OOOOH LITTLE BY LITTLE BY LITTLE BY LITTLE.

CLAIRE. Are you trying to humiliate me?

(The SEXY WOMAN knows she's not welcome. She exits, staggering out.)

DUSTY. Not at all, Darling. I love you, of course. But you have to admit, this is thrilling. Right here in our little hovel, a Who's Who of the "Hollywood Lesbian Underground."

CLAIRE. The party's over, Dusty.

DUSTY. It's Los Angeles, Dear. The party's never over.

>   (CLAIRE *tosses Dusty's pills. She pours the vodka on the floor.*)

DUSTY. Darling, the carpet. Do you know the price of maid service in this town?

CLAIRE. *(Re: Sexy Woman, offstage:)* What about her?

DUSTY. Who? Oh, her? You want to know if I shagged her! I truthfully don't recall. But, come on love, I could use a little in any event!

CLAIRE. Why are you doing this? What did I ever do besides love you?

DUSTY. Love me? Me? All that time I left you alone in New York? Do you think I'm a complete fool? That I didn't know?

CLAIRE. How dare you? When was the last time you and I made love? And in public, I'm still your "dear friend."

DUSTY. Do I need to remind you that it is my career that has given you everything? My career! And do you know what would happen to my career if—

CLAIRE. Your career is over!

SONG: CRUMBS OFF THE TABLE

CLAIRE. And it is not my fault.

>   (DUSTY's *stunned. That cut her.*
>   *They have a terrible fight.*)

CLAIRE.
>   OOH, HOO GET UP IN THE MORNING
>   'BOUT A QUARTER TO NINE
>   GET HOME IN THE EVENIN'
>   TOO TIRED TO MAKE TIME
>   GIVE ME THE LOVIN'
>   I'VE BEEN WAITING FOR ALL DAY
>   YOU'RE ALWAYS A LITTLE TOO TIRED
>   TO EVER LOOK MY WAY
>   YOU GOT ME HUNGRY FOR YOUR LOVE
>   BUT YOU, YOU AIN'T ABLE
>   ALL YOU WANT TO GIVE ME
>   IS THE

CLAIRE.
    CRUMBS OFF THE TABLE
    WHAT YOU BEEN DOIN'?

    WHO YOU BEEN WOOIN'?

    TELL ME, TELL ME
    WHO YOU BEEN DOIN'?
    HEY EY EY EY!

BACKUP. (*Offstage:*)
    CRUMBS OFF THE TABLE

    WHAT YOU BEEN DOIN'?

    WHO YOU BEEN WOOIN'?
    HOO HOO
    HOO

DUSTY.
    I ACHE INSIDE WITH A
        LOVIN' DESIRE
    BUT YOU'RE TOO TIRED, BABY
    TO LIGHT MY FIRE
    I WORK IN THIS HOUSE ALL DAY
    AND I GET TIRED TOO
    THERE AIN'T A DAY GOES BY
    I AIN'T WILLING TO MAKE LOVE TO YOU
    I'M HUNGRY FOR YOUR LOVE
    BUT YOU, YOU AIN'T ABLE
    ALL YOU WANT TO GIVE ME
    IS THE
    CRUMBS OFF THE TABLE
    WHAT YOU BEEN DOIN'?

    WHO YOU BEEN WOOIN'?

    TELL ME, TELL ME,
    WHO YOU BEEN DOIN'?

CLAIRE.
    WHOO OOH OOH
    OOH, OOH OOH
    OOH OOH

    CRUMBS OFF THE TABLE

    WHAT YOU BEEN DOIN'?

    WHO YOU BEEN WOOIN'?
    HOO HOO HOO
    HEY EY EY EY!

CLAIRE.
    HEY, SOMETIMES IN THE
        MIDDLE OF THE DAY
    I GET LOVIN' YOU ON
        MY MIND

DUSTY.
    BUT AS SOON AS YOU
        GET HOME
    YOU READ THE PAPER
    AIN'T GOT THE TIME

BACKUP. (*Offstage:*)
    WHOO OOH OOH
    OOH
    OOH OOH
    OOH OOH

    WHOO OOH OOH
    OOH
    OOH OOH
    OOH OOH

DUSTY.	CLAIRE / BACKUP.
WHAT YOU BEEN DOIN'?	
	WHAT YOU BEEN DOIN'?
WHO YOU BEEN WOOIN'?	
	WHO YOU BEEN WOOIN'?
TELL ME, TELL ME,	HOO HOO HOO
WHO YOU BEEN DOIN'?	HEY HEY EY EY EY!
I SAID I'M HUNGRY FOR YOUR LOVIN'	
	WHOO OOH OOH
BUT YOU, YOU AIN'T ABLE	OOH OOH
ALL YOU WANT TO GIVE ME IS THE	OOH OOH OOH
CRUMBS OFF THE TABLE	CRUMBS OFF THE TABLE

(DUSTY *hits* CLAIRE *in the face, hard.*)

CLAIRE. Goodbye, Dusty.

(CLAIRE *exits, gone for good.*)

DUSTY. Claire! You're right! You're absolutely right! Don't leave! Please, Darling! *(Totally desperate:)* I am so sorry!

Scene 25

(The Source Restaurant on the Sunset Strip, 1970.)

(BOB THACKERAY examines a menu, puzzled and somewhat disgusted. DUSTY enters. BOB rises to greet her.)

DUSTY. Sorry, Bob. Didn't mean to hold you up. Have you ordered?

THACKERAY. I asked the waitress for a cheeseburger. She looked at me like I just shot her poodle. I thought this was America.

DUSTY. That's where you're wrong, Bob. It's L.A.

THACKERAY. Y'know, I haven't been to Los Angeles since The Beatles' final tour. To be honest, I hoped I'd never be here again.

DUSTY. I understand.

(They sit.)

THACKERAY. So why did the First Lady of British Pop exile herself—your words, not mine—to this faraway and cheeseburger-free city?

DUSTY. It does seem strange, doesn't it? I must admit, it's lonely in many ways.

THACKERAY. We're recording this now.

DUSTY. In England I had a network of musicians who understood my style. As well as Becky—and other friends who lent an ear to my troubles. And there were many.

THACKERAY. I've always respected you, Dusty. But I am a journalist, not a friend.

DUSTY. I'm quite aware of that, Bob. So ask me.

THACKERAY. Ask you? What?

DUSTY. The question you and every other journo have wanted to ask me for years. Come on, Bob. Don't be a ponce. Ask the question.

THACKERAY. I see. That question. All right then, Dusty. There have long been certain, shall we say, rumors about you.

DUSTY. Well, Mr. Thackeray. Let me tell you. A lot of people say I'm bent. And I know that I am as perfectly capable of being swayed by a girl as a boy. More and more people feel that way. And I don't see why I shouldn't!

THACKERAY. Well. You certainly answered that question.

DUSTY. Do you realize that what I've just said could put the final seal on my doom? I don't know, though, I might attract a whole new audience.

Scene 26

(THACKERAY *on the phone long distance.*)

SONG: I JUST DON'T KNOW WHAT TO DO WITH MYSELF

THACKERAY. Yes, are you there? The connection's shite, damn it. I said the connection's sh— Look, I'm going to give this to you the way I want it printed. Understand? Now I know what you're going to tell me, that I'm burying the lede or some such bollocks. But this is how the story must be. These quotations must remain at the bottom of the interview. I don't want to hurt the girl any more than she's already hurting.

Scene 27

(Dusty's Laurel Canyon house. She is alone in the dark. DUSTY has a silver box containing razor blades.)

SONG: I JUST DON'T KNOW WHAT TO DO WITH MYSELF

DUSTY.
I JUST DON'T KNOW WHAT TO DO WITH MYSELF
I DON'T KNOW JUST WHAT TO DO WITH MYSELF
I'M SO USED TO DOING EVERYTHING WITH YOU
PLANNING EVERYTHING FOR TWO
AND NOW THAT WE'RE THROUGH

I JUST DON'T KNOW WHAT TO DO WITH MY TIME
I'M SO LONESOME FOR YOU IT'S A CRIME
GOING TO THE MOVIE ONLY MAKES ME SAD
PARTIES MAKE ME FEEL AS BAD
WHEN I'M NOT WITH YOU
I JUST DON'T KNOW WHAT TO DO

LIKE A SUMMER ROSE
IT NEEDS THE SUN AND RAIN
I NEED YOUR SWEET LOVE
TO BEAT ALL THE PAIN

(She takes a blade to each of her arms. The pain seems to give her some kind of release.)

DUSTY.
I JUST DON'T KNOW WHAT TO DO

LIKE A SUMMER ROSE
IT NEEDS THE SUN AND RAIN
OH, I NEED YOUR SWEET LOVE
TO BEAT ALL THE PAIN

I DON'T KNOW JUST WHAT TO DO WITH MYSELF
I DON'T KNOW JUST WHAT TO DO WITH MYSELF
BABY, IF YOUR NEW LOVE EVER TURNS YOU DOWN
COME ON BACK, I WILL BE AROUND
JUST WAITING FOR YOU
I DON'T KNOW WHAT ELSE TO DO, NO, NO, NO
I DON'T KNOW WHAT ELSE TO DO

I'M STILL SO CRAZY FOR YOU, NO, NO, NO, NO
I DON'T KNOW WHAT ELSE TO DO, NO, NO, NO
I'M STILL SO CRAZY FOR YOU

(DUSTY slips into unconsciousness. SIRENS!)

PARAMEDIC ONE. *(Offstage:)* Lady! Wake up! Wake up!

PARAMEDIC TWO. *(Offstage:)* Get some bandages. Stop the bleeding!

PARAMEDIC ONE. *(Offstage:)* Jesus. Miss O'Brien? Wake up! Miss O'Brien…

Scene 28

(Psychiatric ward. DUSTY sleeps.)

(GINI enters, a hippie/New Age type. Flowing dress and unstyled hair, pulled into a ponytail.)

GINI. Miss O'Brien. Miss O'Brien. Wake up, please.

DUSTY. Claire? Is it morning, Darling?

GINI. Miss O'Brien? My name is Gini.

DUSTY. My name is—Mary. They do have the prettiest nurses in this institution. In the last one they were all rather old.

GINI. I'm your drug and alcohol counselor. Your file says this is your third hospitalization.

DUSTY. It may be four. Or five. Who can count?

GINI. You're English, are you?

DUSTY. Irish.

GINI. What brought you to L.A.?

DUSTY. I was following a lover!

GINI. That sounds quite romantic.

DUSTY. Sounds quite desperate, really.

GINI. This is the beginning of a long journey, Mary. I know. I've been on it myself for many years. But if you want to heal, I will always be with you.

(DUSTY smiles. She has a new friend.)

Scene 29

(AA meeting, DUSTY at center. GINI stands behind her, proud.)

DUSTY. Hello. My name is Mary. And I'm an alcoholic.

GROUP. *(Offstage:)* Hi, Mary!

DUSTY. I can't believe it. I am four years sober! *(Becoming emotional:)* Still, I cannot stop thinking of the people I've hurt in my life. There is one person, especially. I haven't seen or heard from her in many years. If she were here—I wish I could repeat the last words I ever spoke to her. *(Beat.)* I am so sorry!

(GINI *takes* DUSTY's *hand. They cross downstage.)*

DUSTY. Gini, I have so much to thank you for. For letting me sleep on your couch, for never failing to pick up the phone, for not giving a shit when your gay flat-mate told you that Mary O'Brien was actually Dusty Springfield. I'm afraid I need to ask your generosity again. I need to get on with my life, and for me that means one thing above all else.

GINI. Music.

DUSTY. And I'm sure, at times, I may slip. But…

GINI. Mary, I'm with you whenever you need me.

(They embrace—the best of friends.)

Scene 30

(Recording studio. The 1980s. DUSTY *at the microphone, wearing headphones.)*

DUSTY. SINCE— *(Stops.)* Oh, I liked that one. *(Listens to headset.)* Yes, Neil, I realize it was one word. But it was a bloody good one. Let's keep it.

(TOM *appears in a corner of the studio.)*

TOM. Always the perfectionist.

DUSTY. Dion? It's been—

TOM. They're remastering one of my old solo albums. My God, I haven't been in a recording studio in—ages. In any event, someone mentioned you were working in here. Thought I'd pop by and see my sister the pop star.

DUSTY. Oh—Dion!

(They embrace.)

DUSTY. Can you ever forgive me?

TOM. Things turned out all right. For both of us in the end, it appears.

DUSTY. Will you wait for me?

TOM. Of course. But Dusty?

DUSTY. Yes?

TOM. The Pet Shop Boys?

DUSTY. Not your scene, I'm afraid.

>   *(She puts the headset back on. This time, we hear the music. She sings—looking over at TOM.)*

DUSTY.
>   SINCE YOU WENT AWAY
>   I'VE BEEN HANGING AROUND
>   I'VE BEEN WONDERING WHY
>   I'M FEELING DOWN
>   YOU WENT AWAY
>   IT SHOULD MAKE ME FEEL BETTER
>   BUT I DON'T KNOW, OH
>   HOW I'M GONNA GET THROUGH
>   HOW I'M GONNA GET THROUGH

Scene 31

>   *(Royal Albert Hall. TOM paces nervously. GINI looks around, fascinated.)*

TOM. Is she often this late? My God, Gini, this is Royal Albert Hall! It's taken her a lifetime to get here.

GINI. So, she'll be here. There's no reason to worry.

TOM. Tell that to the 5,000 ticket holders out there. Tell that to Princess Margaret.

GINI. Is she coming tonight? How exciting. I've never seen a princess in person.

TOM. We're just minutes before showtime. You're not the least bit concerned?

GINI. No.

TOM. I envy you Americans.

>   *(DUSTY bursts in, with shopping bags.)*

DUSTY.
>   WHAT HAVE I, WHAT HAVE I
>   WHAT HAVE I DONE TO DESERVE THIS?
>   WHAT HAVE I, WHAT HAVE I—

DUSTY. Hello, hello! Is everything all right?

TOM. Couldn't be better. Why do you ask?

DUSTY. I've found the most fabulous shoes!

TOM. Shopping, Dusty? That's why you're two hours late?

DUSTY. That was never two hours! Hmm. I suppose it was. But it was worth it. This is The Royal Albert Hall!

TOM. So you've noticed?

DUSTY. *(Very sincere:)* You know what this performance means to me, Tom. After all I've—to sing here, at last.

> *(She pulls a pair of glittery heels from her shopping bag and pulls them on.)*

DUSTY. That's exactly why this audience deserves at least five pairs of shoes. And so do I! Don't I?

GINI. Of course, Mary. You deserve lots and lots of shoes.

DUSTY. Nineteen-Eighty-Seven has been my best year since— Nineteen Sixty-Seven! Even the drag queens are doing me again.

SONG: A BRAND NEW ME

TOM. That's you!

DUSTY. Seems to be my time to sing.

> THIS IS MY SAME OLD COAT
> AND MY SAME OLD SHOES
> I WAS THE SAME OLD ME
> WITH THE SAME OLD BLUES
> THEN YOU TOUCHED MY LIFE
> JUST BY HOLDING MY HAND
> NOW I LOOK IN THE MIRROR
> AND SEE A BRAND NEW GIRL
> I GOT A BRAND NEW WALK
> A BRAND NEW SMILE
> SINCE I MET YOU BABY
> I GOT A BRAND NEW STYLE

DUSTY & BACKUP.
> JUST BECAUSE OF YOU, GIRL
> JUST BECAUSE OF YOU
> JUST BECAUSE OF YOU, BOY
> JUST BECAUSE OF YOU

DUSTY.
> I GOT THE SAME OLD FRIENDS

　　　　THEY GOT THE SAME OLD SINS
　　　　I TELL THE SAME OLD JOKES
　　　　GIVE THE SAME OLD GRINS

DUSTY.　　　　　　　　**BACKUP.**
　　BUT NOW THE JOKES
　　　　SOUND NEW　　　THEY'RE NEW, THEY'RE NEW,
　　　　　　　　　　　　　THEY'RE NEW
　　AND THE LAUGHTER
　　　　DOES TOO　　　　OOH OOH, OOH OOH OOH
　　EVERY DAY OF MY LIFE
　　AS FRESH AS MORNING
　　　　DEW
　　JUST BECAUSE OF YOU,　JUST BECAUSE OF YOU,
　　　　GIRL　　　　　　　　GIRL
　　JUST BECAUSE OF YOU　JUST BECAUSE OF YOU

　　JUST BECAUSE OF YOU,　JUST BECAUSE OF YOU,
　　　　BOY,　　　　　　　　BOY,
　　JUST BECAUSE OF YOU　JUST BECAUSE OF YOU

DUSTY. Ladies and gentlemen, my brother. Tom Springfield!

　　(With some pushing from GINI, *reluctantly,* TOM *walks out on to the stage.)*

DUSTY.　　　　　　　　**TOM / BACKUP.**
　　JUST BECAUSE OF YOU　JUST BECAUSE OF YOU
　　JUST BECAUSE OF YOU,　JUST BECAUSE OF YOU,
　　　　BOY　　　　　　　　GIRL/BOY

DUSTY.　　　　　　　　**BACKUP.**
　　I GO TO THE SAME OLD　BRAND NEW, BRAND NEW
　　　　PLACES　　　　　　BRAND NEW
　　SEE THE SAME OLD　　BRAND NEW ME
　　　　FACES
　　LOOK AT THE SAME OLD　BRAND NEW, BRAND NEW
　　　　SKIES　　　　　　　BRAND NEW
　　SEE THEM ALL WITH　　BRAND NEW ME
　　　　BRAND NEW EYES

DUSTY.
　　OOH, OOH
　　YOU GET ALL THE CREDIT, BABY
　　BECAUSE I LOVE YOU, BABY
　　YES, I LOVE YOU BABY

　　　(DUSTY soaks in the applause. She strides offstage—but her mood quickly drops. She sits down, fatigued.)

TOM. Well, that was quite something, I— *(Notices:)* Dusty, can I get you a glass of water?

DUSTY. I'm fine, really. I think I'm just—tired. Yes, I am tired.

GINI. Dusty, look me in the eye. What's wrong?

DUSTY. I don't know. I'm not well. Not well at all. Oh, Tom. I'm a far cry from *Ready Steady Go!* aren't I?

> *(Crowd noise rises. A rhythmic chant. They want more Dusty! She hears the sound. She tries to collect herself.)*

TOM. Oh, no you don't. You stay right here until we get a doctor. There will be other audiences.

DUSTY. But this one is here tonight, in The Royal Albert Hall!

> *(She gathers all of her energy and rises to her feet—back on stage! She gives everything to deliver this number. But she nails it.)*

SONG: QUIET PLEASE, THERE'S A LADY ON STAGE

DUSTY.
> QUIET PLEASE, THERE'S A LADY ON STAGE
> SHE MAY NOT BE THE LATEST RAGE
> BUT SHE'S SINGING AND SHE MEANS IT
> AND SHE DESERVES A LITTLE SILENCE
>
> QUIET PLEASE, THERE'S A WOMAN UP THERE
> AND SHE'S BEEN HONEST THROUGH HER SONGS
> LONG BEFORE YOUR CONSCIOUSNESS WAS RAISED
> DOESN'T THAT DESERVE A LITTLE PRAISE
>
> SO PUT YOUR HANDS TOGETHER AND HELP HER ALONG
> ALL THAT'S LEFT OF THE SINGER'S
> ALL THAT'S LEFT OF THE SONG
> RISE TO THE OCCASION
> GIVE HER ONE LAST CELEBRATION
>
> QUIET PLEASE, THERE'S A PERSON UP THERE
> AND SHE'S BEEN SINGING OF THE SINS
> THAT NONE OF US COULD BEAR TO HEAR FOR OURSELVES
> GIVE HER MY RESPECT IF NOTHING ELSE
>
> QUIET PLEASE, THERE'S A LADY ON STAGE
> CONDUCTOR, TURN THE FINAL PAGE
> IT'S OVER WE CAN ALL GO HOME
> BUT SHE LIVES ON—ON THE STAGE ALONE.
>
> SO PUT YOUR HANDS TOGETHER AND HELP HER ALONG
> ALL THAT'S LEFT OF THE SINGER'S
> ALL THAT'S LEFT OF THE SONG

RISE TO THE OCCASION
GIVE HER ONE LAST CELEBRATION

PUT YOUR HANDS TOGETHER AND HELP HER ALONG
ALL THAT'S LEFT OF THE SINGER'S
ALL THAT'S LEFT OF THE SONG
RISE TO THE OCCASION
GIVE HER ONE LAST CELEBRATION

QUIET PLEASE, BUT QUIET, QUIET, QUIET PLEASE,
THERE'S A LADY ON STAGE

>   *(The spotlight fades.* DUSTY *has given everything.* TOM *and* GINI *rush to her. She collapses into* TOM's *arms.)*

>   *(*TOM *and* GINI *rush* DUSTY *offstage. Sounds of a British ambulance siren.)*

Scene 32

>   *(*DUSTY *waits in a hospital room.* DOCTOR *enters.)*

DOCTOR. Good afternoon, Miss O'Brien.

DUSTY. Yes, it's quite lovely, isn't it.

DOCTOR. Yes. I have just a few questions.

DUSTY. I'm at your disposal, Doctor.

DOCTOR. First, do you have any history in your family of breast cancer?

DUSTY. Oh my God.

DOCTOR. No need to be alarmed.

DUSTY. Who will take care of my cats?

DOCTOR. We still need to run a few tests.

DUSTY. At least I've quite a collection of wigs!

DOCTOR. A nurse shall be with you in a few minutes.

>   *(*DOCTOR *exits.)*

>   **SONG: WISHIN' AND HOPIN'**

>   *(*DUSTY *sings weakly and quietly.)*

DUSTY.
WISHIN' AND HOPIN'
AND THINKIN' AND PRAYIN'
PLANNIN' AND DREAMIN'...

Scene 33

(Time passes. A doctor brings a wheelchair with an IV drip. DUSTY sits.
A visitor enters. CLAIRE.)

DUSTY. Claire. Twenty years. Twenty years.

CLAIRE. More than that, I think.

DUSTY. Why are you standing so far away? I may look frightening, but I'm really quite harmless. For now.

CLAIRE. I can only stay a few minutes, Dusty. I'm in town to give a lecture at Cambridge.

DUSTY. A lecture! At Cambridge!

CLAIRE. On the history of jazz.

DUSTY. I'm terribly proud of you, Claire. My darling.

(DUSTY extends her hand. CLAIRE takes it — reluctantly.)

CLAIRE. We had some good times, Dusty.

DUSTY. I miss you awfully, Claire!

CLAIRE. Dusty, it was a lifetime ago. Your recovery? You stuck with it?

DUSTY. Does a morphine drip count?

(CLAIRE backs away.)

DUSTY. I really did try, Claire. I tried so hard.

CLAIRE. We both tried.

DUSTY. Then why, Claire? Why did it have to end?

CLAIRE. It was good to see you again, Dusty. It really was.

(CLAIRE walks out of DUSTY's life for a second time. DUSTY softly begins to cry. TOM enters. With one look at her, he becomes very concerned. He kneels beside her, attempting to look in her eyes. But she won't make eye contact.)

TOM. Dusty? Speak to me, please. *(No response; growing concern:)* Mary?

(DUSTY finally looks up at him. She places a hand on his shoulder. She struggles mightily to rise from her chair.)

TOM. Wait. I'll get someone to help you into bed.

DUSTY. No. *(On her feet:)* I want to go to Ireland, Dion.

TOM. Ireland?

DUSTY. I want to go home.

Scene 34

(The Irish coastline. The Cliffs of Moher. Sounds of ocean and seagulls.)

TOM. This place, it never changes.

DUSTY. The sea is peaceful today, isn't it, Dion?

(TOM struggles to hold back tears.)

TOM. How did you ever survive without me, Mary?

(DUSTY looks up at him, gives him the best sisterly smile her weakened state will allow.)

DUSTY. You know, you invent another person, Tom, because you feel like you're not good enough. Then you realize, all along, you actually were.

(She steps forward, taking in the beauty of the sea — and of life.)

Now I have nothing to hide from anymore. It's beautiful to be Mary, to be Dusty, to be a survivor and to simply be—imperfect. That's me. And that's brilliant!

SONG: I FOUND MY WAY

DUSTY.
IN MY LIFE I HAVE KNOWN MANY SORROWS.
IN MY TIME TROUBLE HAS SHADOWED MY WAY.
AND MY PATH HAS BEEN COVERED WITH TEAR DROPS
   FROM MY EYES
LIKE THE COLD, COLD RAIN THAT COMES IN THE FALL.

DUSTY & BACKUP.
I FOUND MY WAY THROUGH THE DARKNESS.
NOBODY BUT YOU COULD HAVE BROUGHT ME OUT.
YOU FILL MY LIFE WITH SUNSHINE,
YOU ALWAYS BRING ME GLADNESS.
NOBODY BUT YOU COULD'VE BROUGHT ME OUT.

I'VE SEEN MEN ON THEIR KNEES COME CRAWLING
AND MY FRIENDS BEGGING A LOT ALL THEIR DAYS
AND I'VE HEARD THUNDER, THUNDER ROAR DOWN
   THE MOUNTAIN, YOU KNOW I HAVE,
AND THE COLD WINDS BLOWING THROUGH THE HAZE.

DUSTY & BACKUP.
> I FOUND MY WAY THROUGH THE DARKNESS.
> NOBODY BUT YOU COULD HAVE BROUGHT ME OUT.
> YOU FILL MY LIFE WITH SUNSHINE,
> YOU ALWAYS BRING ME GLADNESS.
> NOBODY BUT YOU COULD'VE BROUGHT ME OUT.

DUSTY.
> NOBODY BUT YOU, BABY, COULD HAVE BROUGHT ME…
> OUT!

BACKUP / DESCANT.
> YOU FILL MY LIFE WITH SUNSHINE,
> YOU ALWAYS BRING ME GLADNESS.
> NOBODY BUT YOU COULD HAVE BROUGHT ME OUT!

> (DUSTY/MARY *stands proud, confident, honest and real. She exits.*)

Scene 35

(DUSTY *enters, singing directly to audience.*)

SONG: DON'T FORGET ABOUT ME

DUSTY.	BACKUP.
BABY, I KNOW YOU'VE GOT TO GO	OOH OOH, OOH OOH
I HAVE NO RIGHT	OOH OOH
TO TELL YOU NOT TO GO	OOH OOH, OOH OOH OOH OOH
BUT FOR NOW,	HOO
I'VE GOT TO LET YOU GO	HOO HOO
IT'S OURSELVES WE'VE GOT TO GET TO KNOW	
HEY, DARLING	HEY HEY HEY
DON'T FORGET ABOUT ME, NOW, BABY	DON'T FORGET ABOUT ME, NOW, BABY
NO, NO PLEASE, DARLIN	DON'T FORGET ABOUT ME, NOW, BABY
DON'T FORGET ABOUT ME, NOW, BABY	DON'T FORGET ABOUT ME, NOW, BABY

(*Ad lib on repeats:*)
NO MATTER WHAT YOU DO, CHILD
DON'T FORGET ABOUT DUSTY SPRINGFIELD

(Freely:)
I SAID, OH, DON'T FORGET ABOUT ME
NO NO NO NO SWEET CHILD
DON'T YOU FORGET ABOUT ME
YE YE YEAH

(Curtain call.
Music plays out.
Entire cast on stage.)

End of Play

Also available at Playscripts, Inc.

Emma
by Stephen Karam
based on the novel by Jane Austen

Musical Comedy
100-110 minutes
4 females, 5 males, 3 either
(12-30 actors possible)

This modern musical adaptation lifts Jane Austen's comedy of manners out of Regency England and sets it down in contemporary Connecticut. Emma, a graduate student at Highbury College, embarks on a personal mission to set up a lonely gay student named Harry with a suitable boyfriend. She sets her sights on school *a cappella* star Trevor, but her plan is soon complicated by the return of an old rival and a visit from a British film star. Emma's mentor/advisor, Dr. Knight, and her old friend, Miss Bates, join the fracas—and the rural college soon teems with missed connections. A delightful and deeply felt spin on the original.

Cyrano de BurgerShack
by Jeremy Desmon

A Pop Musical
100-110 minutes
12 females, 7 males, 10 either
(19–50 actors possible)

Cyrano is king of the local Burger Shack, but he can't seem to win the love of his best friend, Roxanne. When Roxanne confesses her crush on the new burger-flipper, Christian, Cyrano decides that playing Cupid is better than sitting out of the game. An updated, modern-day version of Edmond Rostand's *Cyrano de Bergerac*, this rollicking musical features hit contemporary pop songs that will have audiences cheering. Songs include: "Call Me Maybe" as made famous by Carly Rae Jepsen, "We Got The Beat" as made famous by The Go-Go's, "Just The Way You Are" as made famous by Bruno Mars, "Firework" as made famous by Katy Perry, and many more!

Order online at: **www.playscripts.com**

About the Authors

Kirsten Holly Smith portrayed the legendary Dusty Springfield in the new musical *Forever Dusty*, which she also conceived and co-wrote and which ran Off-Broadway at New World Stages 2012-2013. Ms. Smith received the Spectrum Arts Grant from University of Southern California in 2006 to develop the project. She premiered an earlier version of the musical, entitled *Stay Forever,* at The Renberg Theatre in Los Angeles in 2008.

Ms. Smith's film credits include: *Curfew* (2013 Oscar winner, Best Live Action Short), *Isle of Lesbos* (lead in award-winning musical, Berlin and other festivals), *Forever Love* (with Reba McEntire), *Firecracker* (with Karen Black), *After Image* (with John Mellencamp). TV/Print: HBO's *Hung* as Kate and the pilot *Sunset Junction*. Among her other theatre credits: *Three Sisters* (LATC); *The Foursome* (Tim Robbins' Actor's Gang Theatre); *Of Mice and Men* (Cape Fear Regional); *Twelfth Night* (Olivia); *Lysistrata* (Lysistrata); *The Best Little Whorehouse in Texas.*

As a screenwriter, she has been twice a finalist in the Sundance Screenwriters Lab. She has two feature films in development and just completed her first EP as a songwriter. She studies acting with Alice Spivak (NYC) & John Kirby (LA). Voice coaching with Bill Riley and Dr. Linda Carroll. Ms. Smith wishes to thank everyone who supported *Forever Dusty*. "We would not be here without you."

Jonathan Vankin is an author, comic book writer, screenwriter and journalist. His work has received numerous awards and honors, while his books have been translated into nearly 20 languages.

He has won three New England Newspaper & Press Association awards. His screenplay *The Tripwire* was a semi-finalist in the 2010 *Creative Screenwriting* magazine AAA competition and another screenplay, *Stay Forever,* was twice picked as a finalist in the Sundance Screenwriters Lab selections. *The Big Book of Bad* was nominated for the comic book Eisner Award and his superhero comics debut, *The Search for Swamp Thing,* became one of DC Comics' bestselling titles.

He was commissioned by French production company Des Films to pen the screenplay *Dragon's Fin Soup,* which he completed with Takashi Miike (*Audition, 13 Assassins*) attached to direct.

Vankin's first book, *Conspiracies, Cover-Ups and Crimes,* was the first comprehensive journalistic investigation of America's conspiracy-theory underground, foreshadowing the current state of sociopolitical affairs

About the Authors (cont.)

by two decades. That book and its follow-up, *The Greatest Conspiracies* series, co-authored with John Whalen, went on to become the most influential books on the subject and led to Vankin's numerous media appearances on such networks as CNN, MSNBC, CNBC, FOX, the BBC and the CBC as well as hundreds of radio stations.

Most recently, he published *The World's Greatest Conspiracies,* the fifth installment in the *Greatest Conspiracies* franchise. He also wrote the graphic novels *Tokyo Days, Bangkok Nights* (which is currently in development for a feature film) and *Tasty Bullet* (with Arnold Pander). His other books include *Based on a True Story (But With More Car Crashes)* and *The Big Book of Scandal.* He wrote the DC/Vertigo Comics series *The Witching,* and an episode of the TV series *The Crow: Stair way to Heaven* (based on the Brandon Lee film).

As a Senior Editor at DC/Vertigo Comics from 2004 to 2011, he was responsible for such series as *The Exterminators* (optioned by Showtime), Neil Gaiman's *Neverwhere* and *Testament* (by controversial media critic Douglas Rushkoff), as well as the graphic novels *The Quitter* written by Harvey Pekar, *The Alcoholic* written by Jonathan Ames and *How to Understand Israel in 60 Days or Less* by writer/artist Sarah Glidden, among many others.

He spent time as a sportswriter/editor at the *Daily Yomiuri* in Tokyo, Japan. His writing has appeared in the *New York Times Magazine, Wired, Salon, L. A. Weekly* and numerous other publications.